# *Self-Mastery*

## The Lost Key to Living an Overcoming and Fulfilling Life

Perry and Belinda Moss

WESTBOW
PRESS
A DIVISION OF THOMAS NELSON

Cover Design by Authentic DNA Studio, LLC www.authenticdnastudio.com

WestBow Press books may be ordered through booksellers or by contacting:

WestBow Press
A Division of Thomas Nelson
1663 Liberty Drive
Bloomington, IN 47403
www.westbowpress.com
1 (866) 928-1240

Because of the dynamic nature of the Internet, any web addresses or links contained in this book may have changed since publication and may no longer be valid. The views expressed in this work are solely those of the author and do not necessarily reflect the views of the publisher, and the publisher hereby disclaims any responsibility for them.

Publisher's Note: This publication is designed to provide competent and reliable information regarding the subject matter covered. However, it is sold with the understanding that the authors and publisher are not engaged in rendering legal, financial, or other professional advice. The authors and publisher specifically disclaim any liability that is incurred from the use or application of the contents of this book.

Any people depicted in stock imagery provided by Thinkstock are models, and such images are being used for illustrative purposes only.
Certain stock imagery © Thinkstock.

ISBN: 978-1-4908-1474-2 (sc)
ISBN: 978-1-4908-1473-5 (hc)
ISBN: 978-1-4908-1518-3 (e)

Library of Congress Control Number: 2013919848

Printed in the United States of America.

WestBow Press rev. date: 11/18/2013

# *Dedication*

This book is dedicated, first, to those who took their lives. We are sorry that you are not here. Had you been exposed to the information in this book, we believe the results would have been different and your life more desirable. To the loved ones of those who took their lives, we are sorry for your pain. We believe this book will not only assist you in the healing process, but also guide you into living a more fulfilling life.

Secondly, this book is dedicated to those whose lives have been derailed because of the debilitating effects of depression and oppression, which often lead to suicide and other maladaptive behaviors. We delay no longer. Your help is finally here!

Finally, this book is dedicated to those of you who know that there is something greater in life and who are tired of standing in the way of what is beckoning you—a life of eternal purpose guaranteed to bring fulfillment in its greatest sense.

# Contents

# Foreword

Have you ever wondered what life would be like if it was NOT filled with seemingly endless cycles of "drama?" During those times, your world seems to be filled with spiritual and emotional ups and downs. It makes you feel as if your life was on a roller coaster. Often times, we unconsciously get on this roller coaster-of-life when we make daily decisions based on our thoughts, feelings, emotions, or opinions. Well, it's time to start living a more fulfilled life. *"Self-Mastery"* is an essential step to making that fulfilled lifestyle YOUR reality. Even if you are experiencing a fulfilled life, *"Self-Mastery"* will empower you to empower others. So, it's a MUST read!

Self-mastery is about achieving results. Documented...quantifiable results. As a youth and family life coach for the past 30 years, I have witnessed tremendous life changing experiences with youth and adults alike. That happens when individuals apply and master self-empowering principles like the ones outlined in *"Self-Mastery."* It is an invaluable and practical roadmap to lead to a foundation for success whether it applies to relationships, finances, educational pursuits, professional endeavors, business ventures, or any other rewarding experiences you desire.

The authors of *"Self-Mastery"* provide us with practical antidotes and personal life experiences as examples to begin living fulfilling lives. Self-mastery is about REAL self-empowerment. The journey to real self-empowerment starts every day. Each day we can take one small step to control and master our thoughts, feelings, emotions and opinions. In doing so, our perspectives change; our motivation begins to go through the roof; and we begin to live life on purpose. What! No more roller-coaster lifestyle!

We are all capable of influencing every environment and situation we encounter. *"Self-Mastery"* provides you with the tools to do just that. Self-mastery is more about transformation rather than *"changing."* Changing suggests altering our appearance or behavior based on the situation or environment we encounter. The down side to *"changing"* is that we maintain the very properties or qualities that created our undesired conditions to start with. Those qualities remain a part of our internal toolbox as a resource that we rely on if situations dictate. Take water for example. When water is heated, it changes to vapor. When it gets cold, it changes to ice. When left at room temperature, it changes to liquid. Water changes its appearance based on the situation it is in. However, its inherent qualities are essentially the same. Like water, so many of us determine our responses or reactions based on our changing environments. What a way to live!

Transformation, on the other hand, suggests an emotional and spiritual metamorphosis in order to experience life beyond our wildest dreams. Take the caterpillar for example. The caterpillar consciously and willingly goes through a metamorphic process because it knows that its life has greater meaning *(Okay, we know it's a natural occurrence but, follow my point)*. A caterpillar experiences the freedom of flight as a butterfly because it chooses to go through certain stages of development in order to discard all those things that were preventing it from living a fulfilled life. In the end, its life as a butterfly could never be mistaken for that of a caterpillar regardless of the outside temperature or other situations it may find itself in. Once becoming a butterfly, the qualities of the caterpillar becomes nonexistent but, rather the butterfly lives by a totally different set of principles in order to live its life the way it was intended. The butterfly now relies on its newly infused but time-tested qualities to influence its various environments. *"Self-Mastery"* provides the reader with those *"newly infused qualities"* that we can use each day. It motivates and inspires you to live a life of purpose and to fulfill your divine potential. Enjoy the read and prepare to soar with your new wings as you shed those things that bind you to earth!

*Dr. Melvin is a youth and family life coach living in Stafford, Virginia. For over 30 years, he has provided military and civilian families with effective strategies for youth and adults alike. Whether he's working with an eight-time felon or an aspiring college student, his life plans involves mastering self-empowerment principles in order to live purpose-driven lives.*

# Acknowledgements

Thanks to Charlette, Sheree, and Vonda, for your expert editing and advice on making this manuscript *Yatteer*. To our daughter Dawn, the recommendations you provided on relational capacity and vehemence that we include a study guide in the book made a huge difference. Dr. Melvin, Dr. Brock, and LCDR Wijnaldum thanks for your inspiring words. And to our friend Terris, we are so grateful for you making it possible for us to get this book published on schedule. The world awaits it and you all made it happen. You all are the best!

# Introduction

৵৹৻

This book, *Self-Mastery: The Lost Key to Living an Overcoming and Fulfilling Life*, is written to help people understand how their personal history has everything to do with where and who they are today and how their lives can be significantly transformed if their focus is appropriately redirected. Many people rarely live fulfilled lives because they allow the crises they face or have faced to become "their life." What a difference life would be if we processed the unexpected events that occur in our lives as events that mature us, some of which occur to make us stronger.

During the Great Depression, many people took their own lives because they could not see past the current events fueled by media frenzy. Engaging in too much negative media reporting is especially dangerous. Everywhere you turn; there are pages and pages, and channels and channels of bad news. It is not surprising that people's hearts are failing them due to fear.

Today, global economic instability, a dismally large number of people out of work, some after spending years and countless dollars in pursuit of higher education, job dissatisfaction for others, relationship problems fueled by, among other things, not enough money, sexual promiscuity or dysfunction, and rebellious children to name a few, have resulted in a world plagued with the highest rate of depression in decades. Unhealthy responses to despair, disillusionment, and hopelessness, especially in difficult and challenging times have become an epic problem; no one seems capable of escaping its grip and no one seems to have any answers.

Unpredictably, in the United States, the Department of Defense (DoD), to include the military, also has not responded effectively to these challenges or these difficult times. Suicide in the DoD is nearly as high as in the civilian community. Daily the headlines expose the growing problem of suicide across the services. Military leaders are stumped at the alarming rate at which American service members and servicewomen designated to defend the Constitution of the United States are taking their lives and at the writing of this book, the numbers show no signs of decreasing. How is this possible, many ask? Quite simply, the military is a microcosm of society. Putting on a uniform does not make one a warrior just as standing in a garage doesn't make one a car. In reality, they are people from various walks of life who entered the service with similar issues as their civilian counterparts. They simply traded their civilian clothes for a uniform, but the issues in their lives remain intact or the same.

We suspect that the rate of suicide globally is equally high, but other nations are not as transparent about reporting their emotional distress problems as the United States, most likely because it becomes an issue of national security. However, the alarming fact is, it's a universal problem and something must and can be done about it. We believe the key is unlocking the treasure of self-mastery.

Self-mastery is about awareness and each individual identifying the root of incapacitating emotional patterns developed over time in their lives and reshaping those patterns to produce inward strength and power. Self-mastery is not about being perfect. It's about acquiring and cultivating skills that enable a person to develop and maintain an emotional state that is empowering in the face of challenges.

It's about developing and maintaining a healthy relationship with oneself.

What most people fail to realize is that pressures in life rarely create the emotional distress that one experiences; it simply exposes the emotional patterns individuals have developed over the years, often times since childhood. When the crises occur, that pattern simply has a face. The distress exposes a way of thinking and processing of reality that must be analyzed. The benefit of identifying negative thought patterns and responses that have plagued an individual most of their life is they now have an opportunity to re-write a *script* that will enable them to pilot their life with a sense of accuracy ultimately leading them closer to a life of fulfillment. That's what self-mastery is all about.

Self-mastery also reveals the benefits of life's contradictions. We all have challenges; it's a part of life. What many fail to recognize, however, is that not all challenges or contradictions are bad and they are certainly not designed to take you out of the game of life. We call these contradictions "Life-Maturing Events" (LMEs). Although they rarely *feel* like it, LMEs are really gifts in disguise. As one grows in life, life demands more responsibility. For example, the life of a single person is not as demanding as the life of someone who's married. When you add children to the equation, our ability to process information begins to affect more of our surroundings and relationships. Without this knowledge, through ignorance, people walk away from the very thing designed to perfect them—such as marriage, relationships, or children.

Personally, we didn't realize how selfish we were until we were married. However, through hard work and merciless internal homework, we learned the value of the LMEs. Instead of fighting against the very thing designed to strengthen us, we conscientiously worked through each LME and now our marriage is not only blissful but also enviable.

Therefore, instead of bowing out, caving in, or ending it all, this book will teach you how to use the LMEs to make you better and stronger.

We believe the information in this book is vitally important for many reasons: not only will it significantly decrease mental health issues such as depression and suicide, or maladaptive behaviors such as sexual assault or substance abuse, but it will also enable individuals to practice state management which inevitably will lead to discovering and utilizing their true gifts which is the catalyst for fulfilling purpose and true happiness—convergence.

Another reason we believe this information is vital, neuroscientists (those who study how the brain works) purport that every individual is hard-wired to operate at genius capacity, especially in the area of their gifting. Some people are gifted to sing, others to dance; some people are gifted to teach, others to be physicians. This is only possible, however, through recognition and cultivation of those gifts combined with state management, a critical component of self-mastery. According to Abraham Maslow, the psychologist famous for the hierarchy of needs theory, an individual will never be happy until they have self-actualized (expressing their gift and passion in a cause greater than themselves). It's what we have all been created to accomplish. Everyone has something to offer.

However, this goes full circle. You cannot ascend the mountain of success without first conquering your own personal mountain, "you," and those things that you think about "you," that are not really "you," but someone else's thoughts about "you" that became "you." One need only take a quick glance at the lives of celebrities who we may consider lacking nothing. However, substance abuse, failed relationships or marriages, troubled children, depression, or even suicide seems to plague them. Why, because mastery on the outside is determined to the degree of mastery obtained on the inside. Thus, the major goal of this book is to assist you in conquering your own personal mountain so you can not only ascend any mountain and live the life of your dreams, but also remain on top of that mountain. It is to provide a key to unlock the door that will provide you an overcoming and fulfilling life.

We are both strong advocates of using self-mastery to promote a life of bliss because personally I (Dr. Moss) experienced depression and suicide ideation for over 20 years. However, we have used the material revealed in this book to become so emotionally strong that not only have there been no signs of depression or suicide ideation for the last 15 years in my life, but we are now consulting and empowering people and institutions on how to eradicate their staggering emotional and suicide problem. A state of "resilience" is an understatement for what we have become as a result of embracing this *transformational* material. We have also assisted in maximizing the potential of thousands of people to achieve the same "empowered" state. Now, it's your turn!

Our caution: do not process this material mechanically or intellectually. We want you to process it experientially. It's one thing to have knowledge of information, but it's another thing to experience that knowledge and allow it to produce "a you" whom you've never known. After all, the end result we're promoting is transformation and change—a life you dreamed of, but perhaps not thought possible.

At the end of the book, we have included an appendix entitled "Chapter Review & Study Guide" which can also be considered "food for thought." It is to be used with each chapter. Each of us has more in common than we realize. For example, at some time during the day there will be many people who order the exact same meal as someone else for breakfast, lunch and dinner. In like manner, our daily lives are filled with the exact challenges, afflictions, and pressures of life as someone else's. It's as if we ordered from the same menu. *Food for Thought* is designed to trigger something in you so that you can daily develop recipes that will nourish your mind so that you can respond to life's pop quizzes in a healthy manner. When we exercise the body, we must always replace it with the nourishment to support us throughout the day. Likewise, we must exercise and develop the mind by living a disciplined thought life.

Now, prepare to destroy any disempowering scripts that have crippled you or prevented you from enjoying life. Your best days are awaiting you!

Perry & Belinda Moss
Smithfield, Virginia

# Chapter One

8—⊼

# Suicide is not an Option

P eople's hearts are certainly failing them due to fear. The nation's fledging economy, coupled with a plethora of social problems has resulted in an unprecedented number of people responding to life in a negative way. The rates of depression and attempted and completed suicides are the highest the United States has ever encountered. At the writing of this book, the latest government statistics purport that 17 million Americans suffer with some form of depression. The most recent study, which incidentally was funded by taxpayers' dollars to the tune of $35 million, suggests that depression can only be treated but not cured. This *acceptance* has resulted in pouring billions into a pharmaceutical industry that acknowledges that the drugs they produce treat the symptoms only, a disclosure that there is a 50 percent recurrence rate, and exposure to alarming side effects, which are often fatal. Audaciously, our health professionals utter, "overuse of medications is preferable than no treatment at all."

Depression fuels suicide to the tune of 30,000 suicides each year, because it induces a sense of hopelessness. Times are difficult, and there seems no prospect of these times getting much better in the near future. If individuals live intravenously attached to CNN, depression will continue to rise, and individuals taking their lives through suicide or attempted suicide will surely follow. The problem is that the media prospers by reporting bad news, and Americans appear to have an unhealthy relationship with the media. The devastating effect of such reporting is showing up not only in our homes and businesses but also, as mentioned previously, even in our military.

One theory explaining the high number of suicides is the "contagion of suicide." In a nutshell, suicide, like a flu epidemic, has become contagious; it has become a viable option to escape emotional distress. In the field of quantum physics (QP), physicists can mathematically explain how one phenomenon can occur in one place, and in an unseen dimension, have the same effect in another place. They contend, for example, that if you take the smallest elements and separate them (one element to one side of the room and the other element to the opposite side of the room), when you rotate the smallest particle on one side, the other particle will rotate simultaneously. If you move them a mile away, one element will rotate and the other element will rotate at the same time. That's QP.

Psychologists support this theory, suggesting that the moment you make a quality decision here, you can affect an outcome someplace else instantaneously. Marital counselors further support this theory, reporting that they have experienced women forgiving their husbands of unforgiveable things, and the moment they forgave them, there was a shift in the husbands' dispositions even though they were many miles apart. Such is the relationship of cause and effect in an unseen dimension.

This reveals that in a quantum dimension, when you go past the physicality of the design, the way that the earth is engineered, you step into a spiritual dimension behind the mechanics. What you discover is that there is no space, time, or distance in the realm of the spirit. That a statement can be made in one place and produce an impact in another place because of the QP theory.

We use this theory to understand the "contagion of suicide." According to a host of researchers in the field of emotional intelligence, feelings are transferable. Something may be happening in one place but affect another individual's emotions in another place. This is what happens when someone watches a sad movie and suddenly finds himself crying profusely. It is because he has connected to the emotions of the actor even though the movie may be one hundred years old. It's because feelings are transferable. Something in him at a very deep level connected with something in someone else. In other words, the person responds because he is *feeling it*. This suggests that people can pick up on emotions the same way they can catch a cold!

Not only are feelings transferable, but people can also become "infected" by feelings without even knowing it. So when you are in the company of someone who is heavily oppressed, stressed, or vexed, or a similar story hits the airways (like the continued media coverage of the suicides in the military), if you are in a neutral state, i.e., apathetic, passive, or weak in spirit, then that person (or story's) negatively-influenced state will start to infiltrate your state. This is not conjecture; the research supports it.

There is, perhaps, an easier way to make this point. You already believe things you can't see. In the physical realm, we have come to realize that there are germs that we can't see except under a microscope. We've never seen them, but because of what we've heard, we wash our hands even though we don't see any dirt on them. Why? Because we've come to believe that there are things that exist that we can't see. Additionally, there are radio and television signals around us right now, whether at a mall, work, or in a house or car, and we cannot see them. In the simplicity of life, the things that have the greatest effect on you are the things unseen: things we call words. Even though you don't see words, they have the unseen power to create an image that can alter your disposition "in a heartbeat," because words are connected to the spirit realm. The point is that no one can tell you how depression looks, but someone can tell you how depression feels, providing clear evidence that just because you don't see it doesn't mean it does not exist. For example, pain is very real and although you don't see it, you can describe it as "it hurts."

Constant media discussion of suicide fuels scripts that "infected" individuals are rehearsing, resulting in acting out their scripts—committing suicide (we'll talk about scripts much later in the book).

While preparing for a presentation to the military about suicide prevention, we discovered a term called the "Werther Effect." It is used to describe the phenomenon that behaviors, whether self-preservative or self-destructive, are copied in individuals by ideas manifested through language (for example, literature or music). The name "Werther Effect" originates from the book, *The Sorrows of Young Werther*, written by Johann Wolfgang von Goethe in the eighteen century, which tells the story of a young man who committed suicide after being dumped by his lover. What followed was an unprecedented number of suicides in Germany by men who were facing similar challenges and were compelled to utilize suicide as a means to escape their own emotional pain. The book was eventually banned.

It is also a known fact that media reporting of suicides, particularly coverage that lasts for an extended period of time is associated with increased suicides. For example, the death of Marilyn Monroe triggered nearly two hundred suicides the following month. In some countries, reporting of suicide is virtually banned. These same countries adopted a journalism code proclaiming that the suicides should not be mentioned and guidance to the editors to avoid excessive detail about the method used if it is mentioned. In the United States, we can really learn something from this.

Therefore, before we go further, this information may be helpful in explaining why you may be tempted with thoughts of suicide. Suicide as a means to an end has become viral, and your present emotional state makes you highly contagious. It's the perfect storm, and all of the elements are present to destroy lives. However, through awareness (knowledge and understanding), you can empower yourself to escape and annihilate the chatter of depressive and suicidal thoughts, gain new emotional territory, and create life in you and those around you. My friend, suicide is selfish, because while you think you will be relieved of your pain, suicide only shifts the pain to others. Those dear to you are left to deal with not only the painful loss of someone they love but also with a bag of unresolved issues that now includes you. We don't believe that is what you desire, right?

The end goal of this book is transformation. We start with knowledge because it produces illumination, which in turn produces revelation—an unveiling of understanding, which ultimately produces transformation.

Transformation is what occurs when you are no longer the same, when something is changed about you in spirit and not just in theory. When you begin to walk in this transformation, you will begin to capture the negative experiences of your past that have stalked you, and then you will see the emergence of a new you. It takes time, but it's worth it!

We mentioned that the information we discovered on self-mastery has "transformed" us into power-packed change agents, living lives of eternal bliss. Now it's time to start *your* journey of transformation. It begins with unlocking the world of emotional intelligence, the bedrock of self-mastery. We are convinced it is not only the answer to each of our emotional handicaps but also to our nation's emotional and social problems. Regardless of where you are or think you are emotionally, the pages in this book will enhance your quality of life significantly. Already, it has enhanced lives globally in all spectrums of society.

(Although this chapter has dealt almost exclusively with suicide as a negative response to difficult or challenging times, there are other behaviors, such as substance abuse, sexual improprieties, or lack of vision that can also be attributed to wrong thinking. Consider this as you read through the book.)

# Chapter Two

⚷

# *EQ* Trumps *IQ*

Most people are familiar with the term *IQ*. For years, it was the most widely accepted predictor of success in life. Those people to the right of the bell curve (pictured below) were predicted to succeed in life, landing the higher paying jobs, while those with lower IQs (to the left of the bell curve) were predicted to end up in menial jobs. What a mistake.

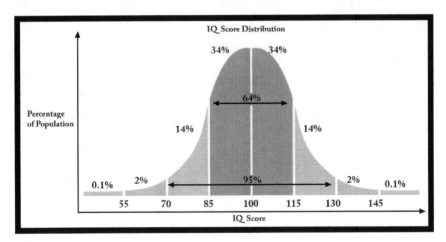

**IQ Bell Curve**

If you felt ashamed because you scored low on an IQ test, you are not alone. Many have felt the intimidation of these and other aptitude tests. A low score on these tests has often left people feeling less qualified and insecure about pursuing certain careers or attending certain educational institutions. However, the truth of the matter is that grades, IQ scores, or SAT scores are unable to predict accurately those who are most likely to succeed in life. Although educators still generally consider these tests good predictors of school performance, a faction of the psychological community is challenging the use of traditional standardized tests, arguing that they are not telling the whole story.

How do you explain when people with a high IQ struggle in life and those of modest IQs do surprisingly well? The entertainment industry displaying a series of criminal justice programs (real and imaginary) suggests that abnormally high IQs are reasons behind a serial killer's ideations. Many of us were amazed at the brilliance of Hannibal Lecter in "Silence of the Lambs" but were perplexed by his emotional meltdown. He was "insane." In reality, many mass murderers and serial killers have an extraordinarily high IQ. For example, Ted Kaczynski, the Unabomber, serial killers Ted Bundy, Rodney Alcala, and Jeffrey Dahmer, all shared a "genius or near genius IQ score." That's why an increasing number of criminologists, sociologists, and psychologists agree that Emotional Intelligence or its casual shorthand "EQ" trumps IQ. It's because history has shown that people with high IQ scores are often stunningly poor pilots of their private lives.

EQ, in a nutshell is maintaining a state of emotional awareness and stability regardless of what is going on around you. Awareness means that even when faced with adversity, you are able to maintain a healthy "state of being" to make a right decision. It means that even though you are in a storm, you never allow the storm to get in you.

Let's begin by defining emotions. In Latin, *"E"* is translated as feelings and *"motions"* denotes movement (up, out, and away). Therefore, a practical explanation of *emotions* is feelings on the inside that can move you in a certain direction. Ultimately, its purpose is to move you in a certain direction. Intelligence is the ability to learn or understand from experience. Emotional Intelligence or EQ, then, is recognizing a feeling as it is occurring and having the ability to make the necessary adjustments.

Self-awareness is pivotal to understanding emotional intelligence. Most people are oblivious to what they are thinking, feeling, or saying and how this influences their behavior. The problem is an inability to interrogate your true feelings leaves you at the mercy of being grilled by those same feelings. EQ is more important than IQ because unlike intelligence, it is something that you can actually develop and cultivate, empowering you to have greater impact and influence over people who may be intellectually smarter than you as depicted on the IQ scale.

Until recently, the value of emotional intelligence training has been a missing ingredient in childhood development. For many, "training for life" was left out of school curriculums. However, the value of this training has ignited globally and is being used in most domains in society with irrefutable results.

In America, for example, many school districts and even entire states currently make EQ a curriculum requirement, mandating that just as students must attain a certain level of competence in, for instance, math and language, they must also master "life skills" for other responsibilities that manifest as they grow in life. Many will grow up to fill vital leadership positions, not to mention the responsibility incurred in the *offices* of those who choose to be husbands, wives, and parents. There is evidence suggesting that helping children improve their self-awareness and confidence, manage their disturbing emotions and impulses, and increase their empathy, pays off not just in improved behavior, but also in measurable academic achievement. Furthermore, this training can have phenomenal results on the bullying crises plaguing America and other nations.

Abroad, many countries in Asia: Malaysia, Hong Kong, Japan, and Korea embrace EQ training, and in Europe, the UK leads the way. Several other countries like Australia, New Zealand, Latin American countries, and Africa, have schools that have also come on board.

This has become so popular that at the beginning of this decade, the United Nations Educational, Scientific and Cultural Organization (UNESCO), a specialized agency of the United Nations, began a worldwide initiative to promote EQ to the ministries of education in 140 countries.

Notwithstanding, empirical data in the area of business successes reveal that with the introduction of EQ principles, leadership skills, interpersonal skills, and ultimately productivity and profit, increased drastically. The Health industry also boasts of the value of this training. Toxic emotions, they purport, "put one's physical health at as much risk as does chain-smoking." Recent data suggests that those who can manage their emotional lives with more calm and self-awareness seem to have a distinct health advantage. It is said, "A calm and undisturbed mind and heart are the life and health of the body, but envy, jealousy, and wrath, are like rottenness of the bones." Those emotions can be destructive if not harnessed, just as fire can be destructive if the burning is not controlled.

An interesting point is that your responses to pressures, when they surface, reveal something very important. It's not the pressure that causes the emotional distress; it's the way you have been programmed over the years to cope with these pressures. It's how you are wired. Namely, it's "your" triad: focus, self-talk, and physiology. Let's begin the journey of self-mastery. It starts with understanding this triad.

# Chapter Three

## Understanding "Your" Personal Triad

One day, during the clean up after Hurricane Isabel, we witnessed our neighbor exploding uncontrollably when his chain saw stopped working. The language that involuntarily escaped his mouth and the demeanor he displayed was illuminating. You see, it was not the pressures he experienced because of Isabel that promoted this outburst; this is how he dealt with any kind of stress. What we witnessed that day was an example of how many people have trained themselves to respond to the storms of life in the same way they responded to, for example, the fear of the destructive nature of hurricanes. Unfortunately, many fail to make the connection to the fact that this is how they respond to most pressures in life. For our neighbor, it was that during Hurricane Isabel "others" got a peek at his previous programming. The storms of life are not going to create your state, they are only going to magnify or identify the emotional patterns that are perfected in you, by you. You have probably heard this saying, "practice makes perfect," and that applies to everything that you do repeatedly; it's called a learned behavior. A person with low tolerance for any type of distress or instability, regardless of what the distress is, will be shaken when something unexpected or uncomfortable occurs. If you are prone to worrying and anxiety, that's the way you have trained your mind to think; when something unexpected occurs, you're going to explode because that is the emotional-response pattern that you have already set up to govern your life.

This suggests that there is a way an individual has been coping and dealing with life since early childhood. That programming is triggered by memories and circumstances. Let's make this personal. Every time you act out a frustrating scenario; every time you give up and quit, and every time you manifest rage, you are simply running the program you've been running your entire life. If you have no training (knowledge and understanding) in this area of your life, you will be held captive to what you have trained yourself to do.

Unfortunately, many of us did not learn this information when it was needed—as children. Childhood and adolescence are critical windows of opportunity for setting down the essential emotional habits that will govern our lives. However, since few of us received this critical data when we were young, we missed out on the necessary tools for growth and development in key areas, particularly in overcoming challenges and developing into strong husbands, wives, sons, and daughters. Instead, we developed a triad that hinders us.

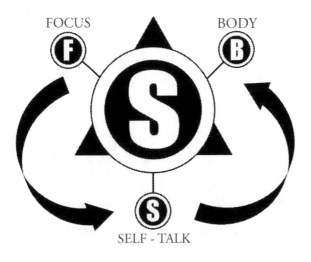

FOCUS        BODY

SELF - TALK

## Your Personal Triad

This triangle depicts your Triad. Notice it's "your" triad—your "self-awareness." It is unique to you and it's been programming you since you were knee high to a duck: an infant. This purports that you are not really responding to situations today, you are responding to the emotional echo of what you experienced your entire life. Your experience now has a face: it has matured and it bears the image of fear, failure, anxiety, low self-esteem, etc. Even though you think that it's the first time it happened (your outburst for example) the truth is, this was a process that triggered transformation (in an unproductive way) through a series of scripts and patterns being developed since childhood. It appeared like leaves appear on a tree as the seasons change from winter to spring, and what you didn't see initially, you now see. You triggered a whole series of neurological associations that are grounded in your memory and rooted in your emotions.

From the time you awaken in the morning, look in the mirror to brush your teeth, comb your hair, or rehearse your daily activities, this triad is running. Understanding your triad will help you discern why your state, mood, or emotional condition fluctuates at any given time.

The triad consists of three entities: focus, self-talk, and physiology: all which run simultaneously and which in turn influences your state or internal reality (the triangle in the center). Your emotional network is designed to be the by-product of whatever you are focusing on, whatever you are saying to yourself about what you're focusing on, and whatever your body is doing to anchor that at a neurological level.

**Focus** is everything; it's what you give attention to or what gets your attention. Most people have no control over (or are oblivious to) their focus; they are easily distracted and seduced. Whatever you focus on gets your attention, and what gets your attention, gets you. This is a critical moment because every thought comes with an emotion. In other words, what you focus on is what you are going to feel, because feelings follow your focus. Your focus also determines the meaning or power you attach to whatever is going on in your life, which in turn determines the direction in which you move. What you focus on affects your behavior. Let's use promotion as an example. Some professions require testing for promotion. While preparing for or taking the test, if you focus on the negative things like your economic status, educational level, social standing, etc.—your demographics—or compare yourself to someone else, you will probably blow the test, because your state will be compromised. You gave power to the negative and that zapped your confidence and ability to perform. However, if you focus on "you;" your diligence in preparing for the exam, or thoughts like, "I've studied, and I'll do the best I can; whether I get promoted or not, it doesn't identify who I am, if not this time, then another," you stand to perform much better. Notice the mentality that was released in you, by you, because of the power you gave or the power you took from the issue at hand. Your focus becomes the joy of taking the test and seeing

14

what the outcome will be. Your state is open and at the very least, you will enjoy the process and gain some new, healthy emotional territory.

**Self-talk** is the "internal" dialog that goes into operation once something gets your attention. It's what you are **saying to yourself** about what has your attention. The mystery is that we are unaware of most of our internal conversations. According to research, most people think at a rate of 1,500 words per minute (wpm) and 80-85 percent of that is at an unconscious level. Consider the example of taking the test. The internal dialog may be something like, "I'm not a good test taker; I always perform poorly, or more profoundly, can anything good come out of Brooklyn, New York—or wherever you're from..." The good news, however, is you have been wired in such a way that your body will expose your "self-talk."

**Physiology** is a five-dollar word for your body and completes the last team player in your triad. We are wired neurologically in such a way, that we have a tattletale available when we are having negative thoughts or feelings. Within a nanosecond, what you think about will always give away your internal state because again, all self-talk comes with emotions that are expressed outwardly. Whatever you are focusing on and whatever you are saying to yourself at the moment, will manifest through outward signs from your body. And remember your body has many entities so the tattletale in the test-taking example, may be something like a frown, creased forehead, instant headache, racing heartbeat, or something as simple as sweaty palms or twitching of the lips, etc. This is valuable information.

Let's put all of this together and explain further how the three factors in your triad influence your interior state (the large "s" in the middle of the triangle). Suppose, for example, that you are going to meet a new person and that person is affluent, or is "important," or has a key of access for your future. If you focus on "that person" and become anxious, self-conscious, or uneasy, then your entire focus will be, "now don't you blow it and your self-talk will be, I need this money, somebody please help me!" Then the physiology of your body completes the triad by causing you to shake, perspire, and stutter. When you finally meet the individual, your demeanor (reflecting your interior state) is one of tension and awkwardness that makes it difficult for the other person to receive what you have to say. If this is an investor, you probably won't get funds or if a potential employer; you may be denied the position.

Let me (Dr. Moss) give you a personal account of my triad: Several years ago, while taking my comprehensive exams for my doctoral degree, although I had completed 30 courses and maintained a 3.93 GPA, my emotional state was tested beyond measure, nearly resulting in me having a nervous breakdown and continual thoughts of suicide. Let's use the TRIAD to unveil the cause of my emotional collapse. First of all, I was the first African-American doctoral student in the program and the first military member accepted in a post-graduate degree program outside of my career field. My focus during the exams was not on passing, but on not failing. My self-talk reflected fears about validating the stereotypes about the inferiority of African Americans to other groups of people, especially in higher education, not to mention my credibility as a military officer. My internal state was so compromised that emotionally I couldn't think and physically, I lost eight pounds the week of the exams.

Although I passed the exam with flying colors, it was one of the most painful experiences of my life. My feelings followed my focus (failure), which was affected by my negative self-talk (disappointing others), manifesting in my body collapsing (headaches, dizziness, hysteria, and unintentional weight loss). However, I am no longer fearful mainly because I am aware of my triad.

Take note of the effect of uncontrolled emotions and their effect on the human body. The effect of a chemical imbalance on the body is tied directly to the emotional state of a person. Again, we can take advantage of this information.

After presenting how the knowledge and understanding of EQ saved my life and is a viable solution to the military's suicide problem, a Military General asked me, "Dr. Moss, aren't you an anomaly? You are emotionally strong and isn't that why you are no longer suicidal?" I disagreed with him vehemently, declaring, "I am not an anomaly. I am no longer suicidal because I used self-mastery to get me where I am today—resilient. It works! Unlike weight-management programs, the results don't vary; if a person uses it they will become emotionally strong." It's because I know how to manage my state that I am resilient.

However, it is important to note that there are some challenges that create a state of unrest that are more serious than others, such as Post Traumatic Stress Disorder (PTSD): an anxiety disorder that follows a traumatic experience, which includes strong emotions that create neurological changes in the brain. Therefore, while emotional intelligence or self-mastery training is instrumental in maintaining an overcoming state, serious mental health challenges such as PTSD may require intervention such as counseling (first) and then self-mastery training, which will be effective. Of course, self-mastery could be used as part of the intervention training in counseling.

If you are a military member or DoD civilian who spent time in a war environment, such as Iraq or Afghanistan, you may be suffering with significant emotional distress, especially in trying to process the experiences that you had while deployed and in trying to assimilate to life at home when you returned. We don't make light of that. We've heard testimonies of military members who have said, "When in Iraq, we are able to disassociate with the rest of the world until we come home, then the demons come out. It's like being in Iraq all over again." Because of the extreme emotional distress you may be experiencing, thoughts of being a burden to your loved ones may permeate your mind. Those are self-defeating thoughts and the number one rationale for suicide. Before you make a harsh, irrational decision to take your life, let's process the origin of those thoughts, and identify the corrupt script in which you are working. Having personally dealt with attempted suicide let me (Dr. Moss) reiterate: "suicide is selfish because while you think you will be relieved of your pain, suicide shifts the pain on to others. Others are left to deal with the painful loss of someone they love; they are left holding the bag and that's not what you want." You want to get rid of the pain. Information is power! Please meditate on this until it starts talking back to you and bailing out no longer becomes an option.

Pain is a great indicator, because when you feel pain (emotional or physical), that means something is out of alignment. Likewise, when you are pulled over to the sideline by an emotional battle, you can process that emotion to come to a resolution. It is important to understand the actions conducted in a battle and the experience that must be captured by the emotional thought preceding the battle. For example, let's say you were abused. The police may arrest the abuser, but you must arrest "the experience" handed over to you by the abuser. That simply means taking the power away from the emotional thoughts that are designed to stalk and harass you even after the abuser has been sentenced to life without parole; the experience if not captured will give you the same sentence. TAKE CONTROL!

You can discern what is going on, but it starts with awareness, not denial, or quitting. Remember, your life goes in the direction of your dominant thoughts. You must change the way you think.

As you become a person who takes command over your state, you become a person who literally has the power to program or renew your mind. That is a state of power and toughness. So, let's jump right in there and discuss mastering your "self" by getting rid of old debilitating scripts and rewriting new empowering ones.

# Chapter Four

## Digging Below the Surface

One of the greatest mistakes we make in trying to solve problems, whether it's behavioral, psychological, or medical, is we deal with the fruit rather than the root. In other words, we treat the symptoms emerging from the problems, instead of identifying what is causing the symptoms. The issue is, if the root is not dealt with, you will continue to bear the same fruit. This is one of the reasons depression continues to prevail as a precursor to suicide and why the pharmaceutical industry continues to make money on "treating symptoms." As mentioned in my (Dr. Moss') book, *Depression Exposed: A Spiritual Enlightenment on a Dark Subject*, while these pharmaceutical companies are making billions of dollars from treatment options, government reporting indicates that 70 percent of the people with depression continue to have unresolved symptoms throughout their lifetime. The truth is most maladaptive behaviors are the result of underlying issues.

We must cleanse the terrain. For example, recently, there are increased findings on toxicity and health-related problems. The studies indicate that many of the diseases and problems that some people have are related to exposure to chemicals and heavy metals resulting in toxins showing up in the blood. Some argue that by a life of routine fasting, for example, one can not only lose weight, but also potentially extend one's life by 20 years. Why? Because as a result of the fast, whatever was in you gets purged—the toxins come out of you.

In others, diseases are the by-products of an unhealthy environment. We fight the diseases when we should be changing the environment. The presumption is if you are highly acidic, then you are destroying your organs whether it's going to be a heart condition, a kidney failure or cancer. Because you are so acidic, you are the breeding ground for the problem. However, if you would alkalize your system, then basically the process would deal with all the potential problems.

Here are two examples making this point more clearly. It will help you see why you must deal with the root causes of your behavior and why you may respond to situations the way you do, and as stated earlier, you've been programmed that way. No, this is not a hypothetical suggestion; you are living a script in which you are totally unaware. The two cases are the New York garbage strike and the AIDS epidemic in Uganda.

In 1968, due to a garbage strike, the city of New York was infested with rats. Rats were multiplying; they were everywhere in the streets and to combat the proliferation of the rats, city officials distributed rattraps and poison. However, they were still unsuccessful in ridding the environment of the infestations of rats. The problem persisted because they were not dealing with the root cause of the problem— excess garbage; they continued to deal with the fruit of the problem— rats. What finally solved the problem with the rats was the removal of the garbage. The strike ended and the rats left because the *garbage* was the *root cause* of their problem.

Several years ago in Uganda, there was a serious problem with the AIDS epidemic. Thirty-five percent of the people in the country were

HIV positive. It wasn't long before the cause and effect of that epidemic began to manifest in critical areas of that nation's government and economy. One-third of the military and government were displaying symptoms of progressive AIDS. Potentially that meant the economy could be shut down by one third and Uganda would have an inability to protect its borders militarily. Ultimately this would produce a destabilized nation making it vulnerable at all borders because other nations would see this as a great opportunity to pick it apart for all of Uganda's assets. What emerged was the destabilization of an entire region and the United States trying to determine how to enter that nation and prevent it from experiencing cultural extremism, communist expansionism, and dictatorial issues: similar to what occurred in Latin America. In other words, everyone was concerned about this AIDS epidemic in Uganda. However, no one had a cure because they were looking for the super condom or super pill rather than what was causing the AIDS epidemic.

The ABC's of destroying the AIDS epidemic finally solved the problem: A: Abstain from sex outside of marriage. B: Be faithful to one spouse and not have multiple partners once married, and C: Use contraception as necessary for birth control and health purposes etc. The result: within 24-36 months, the 30 percent death rate had dropped to five percent. The globe was stunned because the United Nations was trying to come up with the miracle drug or super condom. However, they discovered that the way you stop a plague is deal with the root: sexual promiscuity and poor hygiene.

Likewise, culture deals with the appearance of the fruit instead of dealing with the garbage in the culture. Suicide and sexual assault within our military and among our youth, substance abuse and pornography, and corruption in businesses, for example, are merely symptoms of something deeper. Yet, we search feverishly for the "rat killer and super condom" and all kinds of reasons why rat and AIDS' studies have to be conducted. The problem isn't the rats or the AIDS disease per se; the problem is the garbage and the factors involved in contracting the AIDS disease.

So, let's deal with the "root" of why you may behave the way you do. If we asked "Who are you," you would probably provide a litany of things that you do. For example, you may respond by saying, "I am a communications officer, I am a computer programmer, a student, or I am a wife and a mother." This is not who you are, this is what you do. When we're evaluating behavior, often times we look at the behavior instead of the *being*. Remember, it's the state of "being," we're exploring. To have more, you have to do what you've never done; you have to become someone you've never been. Yes, of course, Henry Ford had a better idea for a transportation system, but people couldn't drive "an idea" until Mr. Ford brought that idea into being: a car. The point is *being* precedes doing. However, don't make a mistake, if there is no doing along with your being, there will be minimal results. However, the focus starts with being. The doing is simply the technical aspects of what you do (your skill).

The following is an image of a Behavioral Iceberg (BI). At a glimpse, what is apparent about this iceberg? Yes, you're right, most of it is hidden: roughly about 80 percent.

## Behavioral Iceberg

The visible part of the iceberg denotes the behavior observed by you and others. Behavior is who you are while you are doing what you are doing. Let's focus on the "be" of behavior. What drives your behavior? It's the first layer below the BI and it involves your thought processes.

Your thoughts (what you think about) drive your behavior. Let me repeat, "Your life goes in the direction of your dominant thoughts." When you look at behavior, the precursor is always a thought and so many people are unaware of what they think about. Thoughts can be murky things and if left undisciplined, they can start a transformation process that will be hidden until the behavior surfaces. You may recall the proverb, "As a man thinks in his heart, so is he." Thoughts are the seed of what a person believes and what they eventually become. Consider this example: A natural seed depends on the ground to bring it into being, while a thought depends on the mind to bring it into being. Interestingly, a seed that is accidentally dropped on the ground will nevertheless grow and materialize because of the ground. Those thoughts, feelings and core values and core needs (which we will discuss later) even though they may be unknown, because they are in the ground of one's mind, will eventually materialize. That's why it's so important to think about what you are thinking about; thoughts are reservations for the future you. This is also important because it is possible that the majority of your thoughts may have originated from unrealistic beliefs. If you do not address this adequately, instead of being moved by thoughts that serve you, you will continue to be moved by thoughts that derail you.

Thoughts are such that within a heartbeat, anything you think about strongly has with it a corresponding neurological feeling. For example, most people are gripped with fear when they hear the word cancer. However, it's not the "word" cancer that brings fear. It's the *thoughts* or *perceptions* one may have about cancer that bring fear. It's the thoughts about people, perhaps loved ones who involuntarily surrendered to the disease or the media attention to the fatality rates of cancer. In other words, the meaning you give to cancer brings certain feelings: fear, despair, hopelessness, or death.

Stop for a moment and think about the type of thought patterns you may have developed over time. Ponder their origin. What or who influenced your thoughts about success, marriage, death, etc.? Are these patterns serving you or are they the culprits for the unproductive decisions you may have made?

Suicide, for example, while finite, becomes a plausible option when people are hurting excessively. The response to hurt is often debilitating when the pain is filtered through an unhealthy "Triad." That's what psychologists call stacking. Stacking is when you are reminded of one failure after another. By layering them all at one time, when you are depressed and things are not working out, this creates thoughts of hopelessness that lead you to make unhealthy choices. Most people are derailed when things repeatedly don't work out the way they planned, and that's when the negative self-talk kicks in and overwhelms them. This makes "what you think about" extremely important.

In European history, the Roman solider had a helmet that was fitted over his head. One reason is just as today in potentially vulnerable sports such as racecar driving or football, helmets are worn as protection for the brain. The head itself has to be protected in a special way. Interestingly, inscribed or etched on the helmet worn by the Roman officers was every campaign in which he had fought and the higher the rank, the more inscriptions that were displayed on the helmet. It was a record of their battle history and a reminder of their successes and abilities; this kept them focused. Additionally, confidence and hope remained at the forefront of their minds.

## Helmet of Hope

Metaphorically, you must wear a helmet over your head. Why, because the battle is really in your mind. Your head affects your thought life. Not only do "right" thoughts need to be in your mind, but your mind must be protected against "wrong" and self-defeating thoughts. Therefore, the helmet is an armor that protects the way you think. If you have a "helmet of hope," you have a confident expectation of how things are going to end up. However, what happens if that helmet of hope is knocked off?

Previously, we mentioned that your thoughts are firing at about 1,500 wpm. At that rate, you will be bombarded with those negative thoughts that are getting in your mind and if you cannot get them out, those destructive thoughts, which ultimately become your beliefs, will derail you. Thoughts, for example, that you are not good enough, or that you're not worth it, create a narrative that focuses in on your present shortcomings and project future failures.

Psychologists use an abasement scale to assess the degree to which people "beat themselves up" when they don't measure up to their own expectations. Sport psychologists also use the scale to assist athletes who may be in a slump. If, for example, a baseball player consistently strikes out, the scale reveals critical information about him. If the person scores low on the scale, they are often sidelined to regain their confidence level. The psychologists understand that until the player regains his confidence, there is no way he can hit the ball out of the park.

Likewise, if a person has a critical score on the abasement scale, the key is to help them shift their minds. Accordingly, if you have a tendency to beat up yourself for not doing something you were supposed to do, or not being smart enough, or not measuring up, your helmet has been knocked off. It is this *beating yourself up* that robs you of your ability to knock the ball out of the park. When that athlete gets into a slump, he *can't* come out of it. It's all based on self-talk. There is a *mentality* of the over comer. There is a point where you get pushed and the stress brings out the best in you. The one who comes out of the slump is the person who has developed an "out of the park mentality." The professional basketball player who has developed a mentality that every shot he takes will score, can go zero for twenty-five and never get into a slump because of the program that is constantly running in his mind. He knows there's another game and he'll go for it again. You must assess *what* you are feeling, *why* you are feeling that way, and make a decision to "come out," and *hit the ball out of the park.*

Now back to the Behavioral Iceberg. We've dealt with the thoughts that drive behavior. Thoughts are married to feelings. Feelings, another term for emotions, of course, are essential. Every feeling has its value and significance. A life without passion would be dull, robbing you of the richness of life itself. What you want, however, are healthy emotions—emotions that move you toward empowerment rather than disempowerment. When emotions are out of control, too extreme, and persistent, they become pathological as in overwhelming anxiety, raging anger, immobilizing depression, or suicide ideation. In the calculus of the heart, the goal is to keep your emotions in check—balanced.

Thoughts and feelings drive behavior, but what drives your thoughts and feelings? Dig a little deeper below the surface of the BI and you'll quickly discover that the filter for your thoughts and feelings are your values and needs.

Thoughts and feelings dictate behavior, but values are the filter that precedes thoughts and feelings. Values are made up of what you believe, what you hold dear. All people desire to live congruent (in agreement) with their values. However, let's be candid, most people are making decisions based on a value system that is not only idealistic, but they are uncertain of the origin of this value system.

If you are a male, for you it may be that you were taught that men are the caretakers of their home and perhaps you lost your job, or are in the military or in a position where you are constantly on the move. What happens when your helmet of hope is knocked off because your belief about being the provider is challenged by these life events? Your state is compromised and the potential for making an emotional decision increases. What about a belief that if you are not married before reaching 30 years of age, you are a failure, or if you do not attain a 4.0 GPA like the rest of the family…you fill in the blank. The key is to determine the belief systems you have intact and begin to challenge them one by one assessing what is realistic and unrealistic. Again awareness is a gift.

The BI reflects values and needs as the filters for your thoughts and feelings. What role does "needs" play in understanding behavior? Every human being has core needs. According to Psychologist Abraham Maslow's Self-actualization theory, each individual possesses core needs such as the need to feel safe, the need to feel valued, the need to be esteemed, and the need to have a purpose that adds value to your life. This explains why a young kid will unflinchingly blow up himself when he is told that he is accomplishing something of great significance and will be bumped up into first class in eternity. If this kid's need for significance drives him, his destiny is fatal. Therefore, there must be a value system attached to that need (what you are willing or not willing to do) to ensure those needs are met in a healthy way.

When counseling gang members many years ago, I (Dr. Moss) recall how flabbergasted I was by the "value" they placed on relationships and the need to belong. When I asked why they thought murder was acceptable as retaliation for a crime committed against one of their gang members, or because their "turf" was disrespected, they responded that no one could mess with their "homie" or neighborhood and get away with it. Murdering another human was as acceptable as stealing a piece of candy. They placed no value on their lives or on others' lives for that matter. Their need to belong superseded any regard for human life. Their value system had been compromised.

One of the deepest psychological needs of every human being is to live consistent with their own self-concept. Until you shift the way that you see yourself and the principles that you want to align with, it's very difficult to have new behavior when you believe you are not consistent with the new behavior. You have to start by seeing yourself in a different way.

Therefore, in terms of values and beliefs, your values sort of act like an umpire on what you think or feel. Your thoughts and feelings direct your behavior. How fast does all of this happen? In the time it takes to snap your finger—in a *heartbeat*. Life isn't working slowly through all those stages. It is not gradual. Thoughts create feelings—fast—in a nanosecond.

The point here is you are motivated by values and beliefs. However, you must recognize the context of their legitimate expression. So, ask yourself, "What thoughts and feelings will I accept? What thoughts and feelings won't I accept?" At the thoughts and feelings level, you can catch whether you're congruent or not.

This brings us to a powerful revelation. Unconsciously, you are living with a script that has been written "for you" from past generations, family history, demographics, media, environment, scars, voices, etc. These scripts are the origin of your thoughts and feelings and your values and needs. The scripts you carry within you define you to yourself. They form an inner image of how you see yourself, others, and the world around you. These scripts are the lenses through which you view your life. Written on the pages of **your** script may be hurt, pain, disappointment, brokenness, confusion, jealousy, pride, distrust, anger, selfishness, hardness; you name it. If you've experienced it, they have become your life script—the way you live your life. The things you believe have become the script that you carry within and ultimately are the source of what you say to yourself—your internal dialog or self-talk.

The challenge is that up to this point you have a lifetime of training that has emotionally conditioned you to certain scripts that are so strong and deeply embedded that the potential for your growth is not dictated by an economy, environment, or personal problems. It is dictated by the power of the unconscious limitations that you place on yourself. Because of the boundaries you've run into, and because of your own personal history, these scripts have a profound influence on how you are likely to behave in a given situation.

Notably, the main script that has the most power is the script involving your childhood, often centering on relationships with your parents and other loved ones. It is the script written predominantly by an *absent* father. There is staggering evidence across all ethnicities, ages, and genders of the affects on behavior due to the father being out of the home, whether literally or figuratively. Often, it's the thing that should have been said by the father, but wasn't said, or worse, the thing that *was* said that *shouldn't have been said.* Then, there's the overwhelming effect of divorce that leaves deep-seated scars in the hearts of children who become adults.

Some other bad scripts are supported by wrong perceptions; for example, a person embraced a best friend or sister more than he did the other or the dismissal of someone because of their weight or height. It's all stored in their script. Another script might be saying, "This always happens to me," or "you see, nothing works for me." It may be a script written by a teacher who never believed in a student—you, or a sibling who seemed to get more attention than the other.

Infants are amazing because they start out with no scripts—they don't have dysfunctional graffiti written all over their brains. One afternoon, we were at a restaurant and this energetic and charming four-year-old girl was having a blast (all by herself). We smiled at her intermittently, acknowledging her independence. When it was time for her to leave, she came over to our table, hugged and kissed us both and said goodbye. Although her race differed from ours, she had no script that identified us as anyone different than she; she saw two friends that she was sadly leaving behind.

That's what so beautiful about children. They are so spontaneous, vulnerable, and innocent, until they are exposed to toxic experiences in life. They must be protected from these debilitating scripts, scripts many of us have not escaped.

What's in your script? The bottom line is your brain has a whole lot of toxic scripting and programming that it will impose on you. That is why scripts are important because you may be living someone else's pain. The good news is, you can re-write or overwrite your script and choose not to agree with the behavior that you inherited. You must change the story to one that empowers you and those around you.

One of the missing links in our lives, and one that can have a dramatic impact on our behavior and deepest script, is Total Unconditional Acceptance (TUA). We are our own worst critics. When some people look in a mirror, they don't like what they see. This may resonate with you. Perhaps you don't like the way you look, your relationship with others, or don't sense any significance in your life. You must come to the place where you love and accept yourself—despite the fact that you have not achieved your optimum goal in life; whether you are unemployed, overweight, married, single, rich, or poor; you must accept you. Stop now and think about a script that you may be running. Is it serving you, or are you serving it?

The way your script contextualizes your needs reveals a great deal about how you talk to yourself. You don't want to beat yourself up because that's not TUA. Anything less than TUA causes you to traumatize the part of you that is most vulnerable—your inner image.

Let's try this exercise: write down three people in whom you feel you can share your most intimate thoughts. Now add a fourth. The first observation is if you couldn't name four people right off the top of your head, you're living more isolated than intended. Perhaps, one of the reasons you didn't have four *trustees* is you're not offering others something that would entice them to want to be in your circle. Alternatively, perhaps you're pushing people out of that circle because you're not comfortable having intimacy. Let's talk about this.

Do you have anyone in your world who really is cheering you on so that you can win in life? In other words, do you have a team in your world? What makes it possible to do the impossible, purport relationship experts, is when you are not doing it alone. When you get with your team and there are others cheering you on, it's amazing what you could do if you have the support of other people. This may be making you uncomfortable because you may be a loner. I'll ask again, do you have a team in your life that you allow to cheer you on? Perhaps you don't. The "aha" for you is that there are probably many people who would love to be a part of that team. It's just that you never asked for help. You have always done what you had to do on your own and then try to give this version of yourself to other people. Perhaps you are recognizing that you never placed yourself in a position where you were part of a team that could help you and probably never felt that a team would be there to help cheer you on. That's programming. There are plenty of people to cheer you on *when you get there*, but there was no one to assist you while *on your way there*. You my friend are missing out on a golden opportunity to excel. This is something for you to think about.

Now, back to your list. The ones who did make the list are undoubtedly there because they give you TUA and you have established rapport with them. Remember this, **R**eally **A**ll **P**eople **P**refer **O**thers **R**eflecting **T**hemselves (this spells out rapport). TUA of yourself and others is essential. You must learn to appreciate your strengths and weaknesses, understanding that each plays a role in your life. However, here is another "aha" for you. Not leading the list or probably not making the list at all is you. That's right, you! This discussion has focused on self-acceptance. The reason you didn't make the list is because you are probably not your best friend. Why is TUA so important? Because how in the world are you going to give love and acceptance away to someone else when you don't even give it to yourself?

By now, an awareness of the script in which you are living should be more apparent to you. The issues you are facing or your responses to situations may be a by-product of your script. Until you learn to discern what's going on and are challenged to look introspectively at who you really are or have *become* as a result of life's experiences, these "hidden" scripts have the tendency to create a destructive atmosphere around you and attract people and things that you don't want. You must choose the right script to take advantage of life or life will take advantage of you, simply because you continue to choose and follow the wrong script.

The bottom line is you must discern the transcript that you are working in your head and how it is affecting the way you behave. What can you do with these thoughts and feelings that make up your script? Very simply, be aware! It is awareness, not perfection that causes growth. The moment that you have a script go off on the inside of you, and you catch it, you're able to put handles on what you're thinking and feeling. That's where re-writing or overwriting those scripts becomes so important. It is the only possibility for transformation. That is why awareness is such a precious gift.

Let's be emphatic here. The real battle is in the mind. That means it is imperative that you change the way you think—what we refer to as "renewing your mind." And part of renewing the mind is identifying the disempowering scripts and belief systems that you possess. Part of discovering those scripts and beliefs is looking at your state (emotional condition). Again, how do you know with certainty what you are thinking with 1,500 words per minute running through your head and 80-85 percent of these words are at an unconscious level? How do you know what you're thinking, especially when in the crush of daily activity and pressure you're not even conscious, you're just on automatic pilot? State is everything and awareness is a gift. Your feelings will always tell you when your *state* is being compromised.

We are often asked how I (Dr. Moss) *escaped* depression and suicide. Let me tell you, I changed the way I was thinking; I renewed my mind, and in so doing I revised or rewrote my script. I now have a new life script; one that is extraordinarily empowering. And I get interesting responses to this, undoubtedly due to the perception of depression's relentlessness. Many think that it requires so much more "doing." The truth is, when I began to practice self-mastery, I released the process of transformation that empowered me to discover emotional and mental strength previously unknown to me.

We've covered quite a bit, so let's recap. Your feelings and your emotional state reveal the quality of your life. It is not about who you are or what you have or where you live, it's about your state of being. Beginning now, you have to stop thinking about how to manipulate the world around you to produce an environment so you can be happy, but rather discover how you can make yourself happy regardless of the environment. Start today doing a ruthless inventory of the dominant emotional states that flood through your being. There is a history to every person and in your history you have belief systems that have been wired together with emotional experiences. All of your "person"ality patterns are predicated on the basic package that you were given in terms of your design that intersects with life's experiences. What happens with life experiences? You have feelings: emotions through events and the voice that you heard during that event determined the belief system in which you are currently employing. Therefore, when you start running into the programs that say, "I can't do this or that;

this will never happen for me," etc., our encouragement to you is to be aware that this is part of a script that was written for you. Until you discover what that script says, you can't rewrite it. In other words, until you know where your thinking is off track, you cannot have a renewed mind. It's about you dialing in to what's on the inside of you; it's about you tapping into the capacity of what's hidden and packed away inside of you, and it's about you going "within" so you won't have to go without.

We have personally developed a list of "I am" confessions that we say daily to keep our mind focused in the right direction. For example, "I am strong; I am resilient; I am victorious; I am full of joy; I am enjoying my life; I am prosperous; I am free from guilt; I am firmly rooted and built up with faith to achieve success..." In other words, daily, we put and keep on the helmet to protect our minds from negative thoughts that would derail us. We command our day with these confessions, **every day**. Let's practice renewing the mind: Take the time to empower yourself right now:

*Tell yourself how strong you are; how capable you are. Breathe in light and positivity. Exhale all of that negative dark stuff you say to yourself every day when you look into the mirror or when you're hanging out with friends and you pick yourself apart and you put yourself down. It's not cute and it's not humble. It doesn't serve any purpose in the world. You don't need to dumb yourself down to make anyone else feel better. The better and stronger you are, the more you are contributing to the world. Don't compare yourself with anyone and say you want to be like them. Be yourself; there's only one you. Your fingerprints and DNA confirm that. If there are two of you, then that's one too many. Stop selling yourself short. We can change the world one person at a time and it starts with you. The next time you think to yourself that "you can't do something; you don't deserve it; why me? My life doesn't work like that...," think about something you did, how focused and determined you were; how you persevered and what you accomplished, and let that drive you; always come back to the best you. Retrace a few etchings in your helmet. Now celebrate yourself. It's okay to give yourself praise.*

You now have some awareness of what's feeding you. Let's take it up a notch and take a look at the most profound and unsuspecting way to rewrite a script. Enter the mysterious and exciting world of "Life Maturing Events."

# Chapter Five

## Not all Contradictions are Bad

You did not personally decide your gender, parents, or ethnicity; you did not choose what country or state to be born, or your personal talents, gifts and abilities. These are all sovereign beginnings. You played no active part in your inception at all. Yet, as we discussed in the previous chapter, those entities played a huge role in who you have become. Likewise, there are events in your life, that you may not have caused, that play an integral role in who you have become. These are the contradictions in life—what we call Life Maturing Events "LMEs."

LMEs are circumstances that develop in your life that are sometimes hard to bear and hard to solve. They are typically areas in your life that are going to stretch and inconvenience you: areas that will initially be unwelcomed. They can linger for a short period of time or sometimes longer. During these events, things are not happening quite like you planned. However, LMEs are extremely valuable. They are really gifts in disguise.

LMEs are designed to mature you. They are circumstances that are useful to jump-start a development phase in your life to move you from where you are to the next level. When utilized correctly, they can move you toward true growth and an empowered state of <u>be</u>ing. Remember, you are moving toward a mentality to where your state remains the same, "yesterday, today, and forever:" an empowered state of being. LMEs take you away from being stuck in your own agenda and your own needs.

In reality, LMEs are the products of the scripts that have programmed your life and have brought you to this event. LMEs test your scripts and determine where you need to modify or totally rewrite the script. They test the "mentality" of the script that has programmed your life to this point in time.

As mentioned, LMEs can be short or long depending on their nature and how you respond to them. If they linger for a short period of time, it is a good indication that you may only need to add software to your script's program. On the other hand, if they linger for an extended period of time, it could indicate that you need to wipeout and rebuild the hard drive.

The main point you are to catch is that LMEs are a part of life. But, let's be clear. We are not speaking of problems or events that you generate because of bad choices or decisions. They are unexpected events that occur in your life that "are not wasted:" events that can be used to perfect you. Sometimes they emerge because your level of responsibility places a demand on you to be stronger and wiser. This is important because if you are really smart, you will be able to know that where you are ultimately headed isn't measured by where you are right now.

Marriage is one of the most profound institutions that can expose your current script. We both agree that we had no idea how selfish we were until we were married. When the honeymoon was over and the "real Perry & Belinda" emerged, we were on our way to divorce court. However, one by one we worked through each event, turning the spotlight on ourselves individually and cooperated with the maturity that was being developed in us independent of the other. Those LMEs not only saved our marriage, but they also positioned us to impact others. We now recognize they were gifts.

So, let's say you are having problems in your marriage and the problems become unbearable. It is apparent that the script you used as a single person is not working in your marriage. You will need to develop a new mentality because if there are problems in the marriage now, and you don't use the LME to mature you at this level, then should you decide to have children, that immaturity will resurface and remain for an extended period of time. Therefore, if the LMEs are not processed correctly or wisely, you can walk away "weak" from the very thing that was designed to make you stronger. Sadly, the LMEs in which parents fail to grow and mature from inevitably place their children in positions to have to deal with the same issues. The children will be forced to conform to a script that should have been rewritten by their parents.

We are both devoted to physical fitness so let's use this example to help you understand the gift of LMEs. Sports enthusiasts will tell you that it is imperative to incorporate strength training (weight lifting) into your workout for weight management. The key is, resistance builds muscle, and muscle burns fat. When lifting to a point of muscle failure, you will feel a burn. That burn is caused by lactic acid and it's burning away the fat on your muscles so your body can transform and become lean.

That's the point we are trying to make about LMEs. Life will taunt you to challenge you to see whether you really believe the dream of who you are. When life pushes back (provides resistance), the real question is "who are you really?" Use the resistance; it will help you become that person and not just have a theory of who you would like to be.

Many of you miss opportunities because you don't understand the process. What's the process? It's what happens *between* the moments of euphoria and disappointment that brings you to maturity. Very little fruit grows on the top of the mountains; the fruit flourishes in the valley. What is it that you're really learning when you're going through a LME? The disempowering script is manifesting before your very eyes, and you begin to discover a script that better serves you. Without this resistance, you rarely see what's in your heart. It is during these times when you are tested that you can simultaneously learn how to make the right choices and identify the consequences of bad choices. You learn discipline.

What does this tell you? It tells you that most of your *Life Maturing Events* are trying to teach you principles that you lack—some values you may need to reevaluate or reinforce. When you get the lesson, your script begins to change. So, if you want to get to your place of peace faster, your focus should be to discover what is the value or principle that is currently being exposed. Typically there is one issue at a time, not a dozen.

To make this practical, let's go back and use the *triad* we've become familiar with to work through a LME. Instead of focusing on how bad it seems or what you are going to do about a failed relationship, for example, instead you ask, "What is the principle that I need to seek right now that will be empowering. In other words, that will keep me in an empowering state? Where do I need to renew my mind?" That's why *state* awareness is so important.

When you're in distress, have a problem, enter a test or LME, what you need is a bigger picture. Why? Because you don't really know what's going on. Everyone has a story. You will rehearse why you are at this place, where this place is, and what you need, but you are unaware of what's going on. You need wisdom because wisdom reframes the questions you should be asking. For example, "why do people always do this to me?" is the wrong question! You need substance—wisdom. Wisdom is the ability to have a true perspective on your *Life Maturing Event*.

Why do you need wisdom when you are going through a challenge? You'd probably rather just have the situation change. But, if it changes without you processing the event, there is no growth and development and transformation is forfeited. In other words, you gain achievement by accident with no template to chart your course in life.

Of course, for those of you with a spiritual background, when going through a process or challenge, you are admonished to "ask of God." So, you humble yourself and ask "what's happening here that I don't see; what's going on that I don't understand; what's in this cycle of my life that I can now mature in so that I don't have to spend another day, week, month, or year in the wilderness aimlessly wandering through life?"

Here is an example of a celebrity with a potentially life-shattering LME, who because she processed it wisely is now living a more fulfilled life. Perhaps you have heard of Adele Adkins, the British singer with the raspy soulful voice. The singer released an album that was 2011's top seller worldwide with sales of 17 million copies: sales, which earned her numerous mentions in the *Guinness Book of World Records*. However, due to a vocal cord hemorrhage and subsequent surgery at the height of her career, she found herself unable to speak or sing and having to resort to writing on a notepad to communicate for several weeks. Having to cancel all her tours for the remainder of the year, there were speculations whether producers would keep her on the job until she recovered. This occurred at the worse time for her career. However, the surgery was successful and after just a few months, she returned to the stage at the 2012 Grammy's not only equaling the record for most Grammy Awards won by a female artist in one night, but also showcasing her voice with such resiliency and grace, that she received a standing ovation. While accepting her awards, she said, "It's been the most life-changing year."

We can experience the highs and lows of her journey. In one moment she was on the top of her game, the next, surgery with prospects of never singing again. Now, after her Grammy triumph, Adele announced her plans to take a five-year hiatus from music to focus on her relationship with her boyfriend, attributing her past failed relationships to the priority she gave to her career. It appears she discovered a script that needed to be rewritten.

Let's recap this profound gift (LMEs) to ensure you get the full picture:

- Life maturing events (LMEs) are like pop quizzes to strengthen and perfect your state of being.
- If everything that occurs in your life appears overwhelming, that is a good indication that there are some weak links in your chain; i.e., the way you respond to things.
- LMEs must be viewed as opportunities to make you better and stronger, not weaker.
- Each time a LME emerges, it's an opportunity to gain new emotional territory that has been lost because of past unhealthy scripts.
- The moment of truth: do I step away or do I allow it to play through?
- It is the law of contradiction in action: How do I respond when things don't happen the way I planned them?
- What is my self-talk—internal gauge reading?

Finally, using your hand, let's present a visual depiction of what is occurring with a LME. The tips of your fingers depict your highs in life: events where everything is going great (you feel on top of the world or simply satisfied; no distress). In between your fingers are the uncomfortable events that occur in your life: all the challenges you question and wish would disappear, or when nothing is seemingly happening—what some call a wilderness period. Now, trace your fingers up and down from the tip of your fingers to in between your fingers. Observe the end result of this roller coaster ride when you successfully complete each LME. If you can't see it with your finger, look at the image pictured below.

## The Crown of Fulfillment

You may notice that this depiction resembles a crown. When you look at the crown, it paints a picture of peaks and valleys. Importantly, what you learned on the mountaintop, you don't lose when you are in the valley. In fact, what you learned in the valley is strength to go up the next mountain or strength to face the next LME. This crown, then, actually denotes achievement AND fulfillment. That's the gift being presented to you when you successfully process LMEs.

People who don't understand that LMEs are gifts, can't understand why they are having so much difficulty. The contradictions are the circumstances that occur in life that shape you to become who you really are if you will cooperate with the process. Knowing this reassures you that during the process in-between "peak" moments, as in Adele's case, there is a latter end. This is the art of achievement. It is the science of how you re-write your script and evolve into the person you were destined to be, not someone else's rendition of who *they* think you are supposed to be. So, you can get to the place where you can TRULY ENJOY THE PROCESS!

You must learn to be calm when you are uncomfortable, because when you don't understand what's going on, that something is being worked in or out of you, the battle in your mind will eventually fatigue you and that can be costly. Not only can "bailing out of the process" prematurely hurt others, but it can also abort the ultimate goal of LMEs: to transform you.

Let's be clear here. What's really happening during challenges in your life? Your script is being re-written. This is powerful stuff. You're being shaped by your healthy response to the problems you have in life. Of course, it doesn't look like it at the time. Whenever you rewrite one of your life-long scripts, you access a whole new level of YOU. But, this starts with "state" awareness and "state" management and there are only two states: empowered and disempowered, resourceful and unresourceful. An empowered state is a state of great opportunity; ultimately this is what we are after. Let's look at this.

# Chapter Six

# The Benefits of an Empowered State

We've come a long way and now you can begin to understand the necessity of maintaining a conscious awareness of your thoughts and how they affect your behavior. What you do is begin to check in on your emotional state as soon as you detect the slightest shift in your state of being. It is said that "the beginning of strife is as when water first trickles from a crack in a dam, therefore, stop contention before it becomes worse and quarreling breaks out." In other words, you want to catch changes in your state early.

There are really only two emotional states: an empowering state or a disempowering state. You are either in a creative state that is open to ideas or a closed state that is confining. People in a controlled state do not have the ability to recognize that being "closed" prevents information that would otherwise be available from reaching them if they were open to receive it.

There are discernible clues for revealing your emotional state. As we discussed previously, you are wired in such a way that your emotional network is designed to be the by-product of what you are focusing on

47

and what you are saying to yourself about what has your attention. For example, if you are frowning and thinking about something unpleasant and asking yourself, "why does this always happen to me?" inevitably your emotional state will develop into a disempowered state and your body will respond accordingly. Remember, your body is the tattletale of what you are feeling. In a disempowered state, your breathing may be shallow, your palms may be sweaty, butterflies or cramps may even erupt in your stomach. You are moving away from life, withdrawing, and are self-conscious. You become totally preoccupied with yourself and unable to navigate through the problem with rational thought processes. You are closed to new ideas or solutions. In an empowered state, your breathing is easy; your head and vision are clear, and you are able to navigate yourself toward rational decisions and healthy solutions. Your state is open! Your focus includes others and not just yourself. You enter a zone, which empowers you to gain the emotional territory needed to create your own oasis.

Now, here's the reality. When you're uptight and you're resisting, when you're operating out of fear, anger, stress, or anxiety, you're not open to the creative intuition of the moment. Later on (after the storm has calmed) you will notice, "I should have done this," or "I should have done that." You will think, "I wish I had said this," or "I wish I had said that." However, you couldn't respond effectively, because your emotions controlled you and you "couldn't see the forest for the trees." What you must learn to do is arrest the episode in the moment—at the beginning before it takes root.

Your state produces openness or constriction, creativity or destructiveness. Have you seen the television game show Family Feud? In the bonus round of the game, the contestant has minimal time to answer spontaneously questions posed by the host. The question is something like, "name a state beginning with the letter "W." Oh, that's a slam-dunk to those of us watching it at home because there is no pressure on our performance—Washington we bellow confidently. However, when other variables are involved like nerves, doubt, fear of failure, or the fact that $20,000 is at stake, all happening in a nanosecond for the contestant, that emotional state can become closed and the mind blocked. When you hear the contestant respond with something ridiculous like District of Columbia. District of Columbia, you shriek. "What were they thinking?" It's not that the correct response was not in their minds somewhere, their emotional state was compromised due to the variables mentioned previously and the correct response was blocked from getting through. This is what happens when you are in a closed state. Instead of walking away with $20,000, you walk away with nothing except baggage (poor self-talk).

Here's another example: make a tight fist with your left hand. Now take the index finger of your right hand and try to force it into and through your tightly closed fist. Come on, push it through. Are you noticing that it is not easy to get your finger through your tightly closed fist? Now loosen up your fist and push your index finger through it. Keep loosening it up, if necessary, and keep pushing the index finger through it. The reality is when you are uptight and resisting, you're not open to the correct wisdom for the situation at hand. If you are tight, you lose the benefit of gaining insight that would have become a permanent part of your life. It's almost like there is an idea trying to get there, trying to get through to you, but it cannot prevail.

Here is a more practical example. Let's say that you are in an argument with your spouse, when your state is closed, that small still voice begging you to keep quiet or say something edifying, can't get through because you are being controlled by the loud voice of your self-talk. So, instead of creating an environment of peace, you become abrasive and enough of these incidents eventually lead you to divorce court or something more devastating. What would happen if you were more aware of your state and how to respond when your state is compromised? That's what self-mastery is all about my friend.

So, what action do you take when your state is closed? Become aware and get loose. You have to shift your focus on what's happening. It's a gift even though it's not easy to see it that way in the beginning. Awareness alone is truly a gift, what you do with that awareness can transform your life.

You must be able to assess what state you are in, in a heartbeat. If you are operating in a state that is not producing the results you desire, you must begin to run your personal checklist: "where are my thoughts; where am I going; what are my feelings revealing to me about me, and where is my mind taking me?" Then interrupt the pattern and begin to establish a new pattern that we refer to as "disciplining your thought life."

How long does it take you to go from a state of unrest—depression, anxiety, fear, heaviness, sorrow and bitterness, etc., into a state of harmony? You can access an empowered state in a heartbeat because it's a matter of switching from one state to the next. When do you want to do that? You want to do this anytime your state has been compromised—the moment that you are not in an empowered state. Immediately, your response must be to return to a state where you're creative, hearing, and making rational and wholesome choices. It is vitally important to understand that your emotions should not be allowed to make your decisions, rather your decisions should create the atmosphere you desire.

What do you believe you must possess or do to access an empowered state? Most people have rituals they have developed over the years (e.g., the right environment, everyone must be out of the house, drugs or a Macchiato from Starbucks). The reality is you don't have to go anywhere to get there or rely on an outside source to get you there. Once you begin to practice a new script by renewing your thinking, you can access your desired state at a moment's notice. Every state can be changed the moment you change what you are focusing on and what you do with the information you are receiving. One of the most powerful ways to shift your state is to ask yourself an empowering question. For example, "what would the empowering response be to this situation?" Initially this task may take longer, but as you work the process, particularly through awareness, you will see just how easy it is. Let's end this chapter with some clear examples of how easy it is to change your state:

(a) You come home from a long day and need a nap just before dinner. You tell the kids to be quiet so you can get some rest, only to be awakened by a loud screeching voice. You jump out of bed frantically to put an end to this open rebellion only to find that your child's finger got shut in the door. Result: instantaneous state change. Clue: all of that energy was based on a focus that was inaccurate. Once the focus changed, your physiology and actions changed.

(b) You receive a call from a relative who only calls when he wants something. Immediately you're tense because you've made the decision not to bail him out again and are somewhat apprehensive about how he will react. This time, however, he's calling to tell you of an epiphany he had the day before about your consistent display of Total Unconditional Acceptance (TUA) to him. Result: instant state change.

(c) You're enjoying some bonding time with the family when the doorbell rings. You think it's a salesperson ignoring the "no soliciting" sign visibly displayed outside your door—right next to the bell. You go to the door with fire in your eyes, only to find it's the Prize Patrol from Publishers Clearing House with your million-dollar check. Result: instant state change.

The acid test for determining your emotional health or maturity is how long it takes you to get back to a resourceful state once it has been or is being compromised. How long does it take you to go from a state of unrest—depression, anxiety, fear, heaviness, sorrow and bitterness, etc., into a state of peace? Again, snap your fingers. That's how long it takes. You can access an empowered state in a *heartbeat* because it's based on the information you are processing. However, it takes practice, practice, practice.

You say, yeah, Mosses, that's easier said than done. Oh no! What happens if you are in a heated argument with your spouse and your supervisor shows up unexpectedly or in the middle of your "intense fellowship" the phone rings and it's your Pastor, Priest or Rabbi..., yep, instant state change. Case closed!

Here's the point, the moment you acquire information to change your focus, your state changes. This is what we want you to catch: your entire emotional state is dominated by your focus at any moment and the moment you get new information, your whole state changes automatically. The key is to work "the triad." If you are not in a resourceful state, immediately allow that to be the opportunity to change your focus, which is your invitation to change your state. Of course, that deeply embedded script is the anchor for your triad so let's get to work and break the pattern of past negative programming.

# Chapter Seven

# The Triad of Transformation

While briefing a group of military leaders concerning their resiliency program to combat suicide in the military, we concluded that their program was not memorable; it had no stickiness factor; it didn't pierce the heart of the target population—the personnel contemplating suicide. The idea is you want a message that others can internalize, that's what makes it viral; what makes it spread, penetrable, and sticky. What do we mean by sticky? The message must make an impact; it must make an impression that sticks in the mind of people; they can't get it out of their head; it sticks in their memory. This is what their program lacked. Their resiliency program is packed with information only and the participants have no "experience" with the material, so the problem of suicide and suicide ideation persists.

Consequently, our goal for this book is not to simply provide you with yet another theory on behavioral change—that has no stickiness. The goal is to bring transformation. "Knowledge brings illumination which brings revelation—an unveiling of something, which ultimately brings transformation." As we said previously, transformation is what occurs when you become someone you have never been before; when something is changed about you behaviorally, not theoretically.

Farming principles are a good way to understand the process of transformation that we're purporting. Before an apple seed can manifest apples, it must transform into a mature apple tree; only then will apples appear. Just as every seed produces after its kind, every thought produces after its kind. Why? Because it is a law of nature that whatever *you are* materializes and what materializes is a reflection of what you believe as your truth (seed). When you are proceeding long enough in that transformation process, you will see a demonstration of change because every seed goes through a process of transformation before its intended fruit manifests. A thought process maintained long enough will eventually transform a person's behavior.

You my friend can change. When facing the need to change, many are "stuck," simply because they don't believe they can change or because they believe, "it's in my blood; it's who I am," or "it's in the cards." That's why many people never lose weight, even when that weight makes them unhealthy. They surrender their obesity to genetics, subconsciously accepting and practicing eating habits that promote obesity all their lives. But that's simply not true. You can reshape your body, no matter your age or size. Likewise, you do not have to remain the same emotionally; you do not have to remain a product of your environment; you can re-program your thinking.

Real mastery in any profession is the ability to make greater and finer distinctions than other people, i.e., the mastery of a cardiologist exceeds that of a gynecologist; the mastery of a brain surgeon exceeds that of an ear, nose, and throat specialist. Mastery is measured by your ability to make better distinctions in decision-making. The more vocabulary you have, the more it reflects your mastery of a subject, because distinctions are made as a result of mastery in that arena. We want you to achieve self-mastery. As you will discover in the final chapter, the sooner you master your personal mountain—you—the closer you get to self-actualization. Self-actualization is the place where your gifts, talents, and acquired skills combine with your ultimate sense of purpose. It's where you get a role that matches you. So let's get busy.

We've learned that the responses to pressures in one's life reveal the programming one has been running since childhood. Now that you have been empowered with that understanding, you can begin the process of breaking the patterns of negative past programming and live a more fulfilled life. You start by accepting personal responsibility and becoming the pilot of your own life. You can use the knowledge gained about your *triad* to produce this transformation.

The first component of the Triad of Transformation is *State Management*. State management is about recognizing your current state when it is compromised and doing what's necessary to return to an empowered state. It is owning all of your emotional territory, whether you are in the valley, or whether you are on the mountaintop. State Management, however, starts with self-awareness.

Self-awareness is a gift. Why? Because once you know how you're wired, **you** can manage **you**. It's self-mastery. Awareness is not only awareness of your emotional state, but ultimately, it includes an awareness of who you are; i.e., what makes you "you," your strengths and your limitations. Are you aware of your undeveloped areas? Are you aware of how you are coming across when you interact with people?

Self-awareness is the ability to be objective about yourself; to step away from yourself and observe "you" from a third party's point of view. **You** must discern your own internal state. Your present state is your invitation to look at state management. Make a practice of checking in on your state and using your triad (focus, self-talk, and physiology) to analyze "why" you are feeling what you are feeling. If you don't manage it, it will manage you. Practice catching yourself as your mind wanders; see where it's attempting to make reservations for you in the future. If your mind is wandering, follow it (figuratively). If you begin to feel some discomfort, i.e., your peace is being compromised, or you're feeling pain (remember all pain whether physical or emotional is a sign that something is out of alignment), at that moment, "freeze frame" and don't ignore it. Don't budge until you have resolved what or "who" is talking to you at that moment; what is compromising your state; what viral script are you rehearsing? Don't allow yourself to get away with anything. At any moment, observe your state; stop and check in—analyzing and disciplining yourself if necessary. The key is you must catch it in the moment that it is occurring—in the beginning. Then, do the work by opening your mouth and subdue that defeating self-talk and *don't be afraid to talk to yourself—you're doing it anyway—that's what self-talk is. You're simply doing it audibly so you can hear your own empowering words.* Echo words that will get you out of that state, not words driven by unhealthy emotions. You want to focus on words based on your understanding. If the environment is not conducive to speaking audibly to challenge the self-talk (i.e., others are around), make a mental note—give yourself a thumbs up, sort of like in the movie *Avatar*, it's like saying, "I see you." This practice has become a part of how we live. For example, if we receive a negative report, (text, telephone call, email, physician's diagnosis, etc.), or find ourselves in an uncomfortable environment that leaves us feeling less than optimal, we immediately run the triad. We start the regimen of questions: "Okay, what's my focus; what is the meaning I'm giving to this issue; what is the unconscious chatter?" Bingo! Once you expose this (and it can be done in a heartbeat), you can breathe a sigh of relief because not only will you return to a resourceful state, you've uncovered additional parts of that script that has wreaked havoc in your life and now it's changing.

The person who knows how to manage his state has developed a voice of truth in his heart. This means he is learning how to control the scripting that is navigating his mind and his emotions when something is trying to divert or capture his focus. For example, your spouse is being unreasonable, or your supervisor "gets on your nerves" or you continue to come up short financially at the end of the month. When you develop self-mastery, you control your focus and internal dialog; you don't yield your mind to anger, fear, or self-pity. You are aware of what's going on and avoid being swept with a tremendous velocity. This is how individuals "go postal." It happens quickly. Really, friend, this is where you've missed it (we certainly had) because most people are not examining what thoughts are going through their minds. Rather, they get stuck in the current and live a life of facades and emotional roller coaster rides, daily, without going to an amusement park (without leaving home).

By managing your state you can live in a bubble of your wise choices because **you** can choose what **you** focus on and what **you** say to yourself and therefore, experience the feelings and emotions that accompany those choices. Again, it's important to remember that you are not moved based upon how you feel, but based upon who and what you understand. This is called taking *Personal Responsibility*, the catalyst to transformation and the second component of the triad.

Personal responsibility is the conviction to control all of your emotional territory. For example, if you take only 99 percent *personal responsibility* for your emotions, one percent of your emotional territory belongs to someone else. That one percent can have a profound effect on your state management.

The first rule is that you must take 100 *percent responsibility* for your current state. At no point can you afford the luxury of surrendering the power of the control of your state to any outside force (your past, spouse, children, a family member, co-worker, the fledgling economy, world events or political developments, an irate or discourteous driver—not even your priest, rabbi, or pastor), nothing and no one. Why? Because that's the essence of being held hostage. The moment you surrender your state by **any percentage** to **any** outside force, you've surrendered your personal power. Your disposition must be to take 100 percent responsibility for everything that you're thinking, seeing, saying, feeling, and doing regardless of the circumstances. You refuse to surrender the option of your feelings or thinking to any force outside your control. Either you own 100 percent of you, or you leave a percentage open for someone else to own. This redundancy is on purpose because you must get this! Our spiritual mentor says it this way, "it doesn't matter how anyone treats you, but how you treat them." I would add, "or how you respond to how they treat you." Remember, "sticks and stones may break your bones, but words will never hurt you," unless you rehearse and believe them. That's a powerful statement because *what* happens to you in life is not as important as *how* you respond to what happens to you in life.

No matter what, you must never resort to a victim's mentality. In other words, if you are wronged, falsely accused, betrayed, disrespected even by your spouse, children, or family member or friend, you take 100 percent responsibility for YOU. You must learn to swear to your own hurt and remain resilient. Your focus and self-talk cannot be "how can this person (s) do that to me?" etc., as that thought is taking you somewhere and besides, sometimes your conclusion may be unfounded. You cannot have a victim's mentality, ever. Trust me, this will not only save you from hardships, it will add years worth living to your life and will lead to a greater level of *personal responsibility.*

You know that you're taking personal responsibility when you continue to ask mature questions like, "What am I responsible for? Can I govern or change my behavior? What is my flexibility in being able to take responsibility for undeveloped areas and doing what's necessary to develop them? Do I have the ability to identify what's happening when I am with people and able to adjust myself so I can achieve the right results?" Right results contain the capacity to empower everyone in the process, if they too are willing to change. "Do I have the ability to respond to situations flexibly so I can adjust myself to get a different outcome?"

The third component in the triad of transformation is *Sustained Motivation*. Sustained motivation is being able to keep yourself on the task or the assignment without changing. Why is sustained motivation a self-mastery skill? Because it's easier to start out with great motivation or enthusiasm with something, but it's hard to finish especially when challenged with a Life Maturing Event. The famous Marshmallow Test explains this component more clearly.

Researchers used the Marshmallow Test to determine the emotional intelligence level of individuals. They tracked students from age eight until they were around twenty-three, in order to evaluate their career track and success level based upon their ability to handle marshmallows. When the kids were eight years old, the researchers placed them in a room, put a marshmallow in front of them and explained to them that if they could delay gratification (an aspect of sustained motivation), when the researcher returned later, they would give them an additional marshmallow. However, if the students couldn't delay gratification, they could just eat the marshmallow now, but they would not receive any additional ones. The study revealed that the students who did not eat the marshmallow (delayed gratification), when tracked over the years, were on the whole averaging 50 percent more accumulation of money and income than the children who couldn't wait five to ten minutes.

During the study, the researchers had a hidden camera where they watched the children while they couldn't eat the marshmallows. One child walked away from the marshmallow and began hitting his head on the wall, but he beat the Marshmallow Test and ended up achieving more significant career advancement on the whole. The students who delayed gratification were 75 percent more advanced in their careers by their own definition and more fulfilled than the students that ate the marshmallow. The point is how much can you handle delay in order to get something better? You can use this knowledge in processing through a LME. If you can delay your need for a reward or certain feeling until the Life Maturing Event is over, your end result will be better than the beginning. Here's a great example of sustained motivation:

"A young man was working on a project for a doctoral thesis in math. He performed statistical studies of satisfaction in business attempting to find the key to job satisfaction. He selected a company in Connecticut, interviewing the employees in the stockroom. Everyone was miserable; they didn't like working for the company because they had management problems. He interviewed middle management and they didn't like the employees because of union problems. He interviewed upper management and the owner wanted to sell the company because they considered it a hassle working in that place. He finished his survey realizing that the data revealed that no one liked their job. Then he hears a person whistling: it's the janitor. He finds the janitor; he's whistling with his headphones on and seems to be having a private party. The researcher asks him how long he had been working for the company. He responded six years. He asked him about his satisfaction while working for the company. The janitor says he loves it and when asked why he is so happy when everyone else is miserable, he discovers that the janitor had a vision for where he was going in the future and was connecting the money he was making from this job to the vision he had when he completed law school which he was attending at night. He and his wife had a plan. He was connecting the mundane moment to the purpose of where he was going. He had sustained motivation. Where he was headed in his heart fueled where he was right now. He optimized sustained motivation; a precursor for transformation."

Those lacking in sustained motivation avoid the process of transformation because they believe they have no purpose in life and they have nothing to offer. Consequently, their decisions are connected to a life that does not require changes because they take what life gives them. At the end of the day, what you want is a high *EQ*. What are the criteria for a high EQ? Those with high levels of emotional intelligence (EQ) have the ability of *sustained motivation* and *personal responsibility*—in that they can adjust themselves based on sensory acuity which means they keep taking in data and keep scanning and adjusting—and they *are totally self aware*. This is where you're headed as you approach the end of this book.

An important element often overlooked in the transformation process, is the use of your body. As we mentioned previously, asking yourself empowering questions about the situation can alter your state. Another powerful way to shift your state is to do something with your body. Changing your physiology is one of the fastest and most effective ways to alter your state (if it is to be a genuine change). Let's take a look.

# Chapter Eight

8━🗝

# Honor your "Body" as a Weapon

**M**artial artists undergo a grueling physical regimen not just for self defense, but to build strength, stamina, and flexibility in mind, body, and spirit. This is designed to hone the mind, body, and spirit. They have learned that to be highly resilient is to harmonize in all three areas. Likewise, for an overcoming life, your spirit (heart), soul (mind, will, and emotions), and body must work harmoniously if you are going to remain in an empowered and open state. Your body can become a weapon in your warfare against adversity or your body can become your enemy if you don't learn how to live a disciplined thought life. What are you demonstrating with *your* body? Additionally, as we stated earlier, toxic emotions put your physical health at as much risk as does chain-smoking. Recent data suggests that those who manage their emotions develop a mentality that produces longevity. It is said, "A sound mind makes for a robust body, but runaway emotions corrode the bones."

Many are familiar with toxic goods and the damage it does to the body, but what about "toxic thoughts?" Toxic thoughts can throw the body into a chemical imbalance. There is a clear danger to the health of your body when you don't take 100 percent responsibility for your state and become a victim of uncontrolled emotions.

The brain is designed to release the chemical endocrine, to support whatever emotional signal it receives from the heart—not the physical organ, your spirit. The heart is the production center that determines the course of your life; it's your mentality software. A constant state of uncontrolled emotions affects both your mental and physical health. No thought should enter into your mind uncontested; it must be disciplined and when necessary, changed to produce the emotional state that keeps you empowered at all times.

The key is to honor your body as a weapon. It is as much a part of your arsenal in warfare as your spirit is in remaining strong. Your body must reflect the message that's on the inside of you. In other words, saying you are happy in a slumped posture void of energy, is an incongruent testimony.

What you do with your body has a direct relay message with your brain in terms of your current emotional state. That is to say, your body doesn't lie; it's the tattletale. Your body is so wired to the spirit of your mind, that what you do physically connects with a neurological system that supports or contradicts your purpose. Your very disposition can cause you to triumph or fail. The point is, if you want your triad to be on the same page triumphantly, you have to take ownership of what you do with your body not only biochemically (what you eat—you can't abuse your body and expect to be an over comer), but also how you manage your physiology.

Let's examine your face to make this point more definitively. You have about 80 muscles in your face and what you think, choose, and feel, wires a message to your brain as to what's happening. In other words, when you smile, it is because of the contents of the information chosen and the emotions attached to it that sends a message to your brain that says something's up. And when you frown, it is because you sent a message to your brain that says something's down. If you ask someone how they are doing, watch their entire physiology when they respond. Their physiology will give them away. It makes no sense to say you have peace if physiologically, the 80 muscles in your face reflect something totally inconsistent.

Have you considered why some individuals are attracted to some people and not to others? People who have mastered their physiology and emotional and internal state attract people to them because strength is congruently being communicated to them by their behavior. Likewise, people who have not mastered their physiology repel most people. That means when people look at you, they ought to be able to do a scan and get an impression of what you're really like. Make sure you send a message that is congruent with whom you really are. And the key is not to try to fake it so no one will know how you really feel. As the famous quote from Shakespeare's Hamlet states, "To thine own self be true." It's time for the authentic you to "show up" and not someone else's rendition of you.

Once again, the objective here is self-awareness. Recognize what is within you (provided you have worked the processes) and that you have access to it instantly. Immediately assess your state and make the necessary adjustment. Bring your body in line with your spirit and not with the emotions that you are experiencing, especially if they are toxic. Swift adjustments will yield amazing results; you will not only become resilient, but get closer to discovering who you really are. The secret to remaining resilient is learning to bring your mind and body under the discipline of your "strong" spirit until you become unmovable and unshakable in the face of adversity.

We're finally nearing the end of this book. With just one more piece of information remaining to help you live a more productive life, take a moment to reflect on what you've read so far. Don't move too quickly through the information presented. Be sure to stop and process the dialog, especially when you discover that it is exposing the scripts that you never knew existed or when you feel an emotional pull to give up and quit because you think you're too old or exhausted to learn the lines of a new script. It simply reveals that you have a crack in your helmet. That's the point. You need a new helmet and this information is designed to give you exactly that.

There is a great life ahead of you, but it's not until you take on your "own" personal mountain—you. We have discovered that if you don't purposely work at being resilient, strong, or establishing a high EQ; if you don't make a decision that you can indeed be triumphant in every area of your life, you will continue to faint in the day of adversity. Tragically, you'll miss out on the greatest opportunity for convergence: that place where your gifts, talents, and acquired skills combine with your ultimate sense of purpose and passion, releasing you for a role in life that is so much greater than you. And that my friend defines fulfillment. The fascinating fact is, your very design (how you are soft and hardwired) is the catalyst for this achievement. This leads us to our final thought: you are wired to excel.

# Chapter Nine

## Wired for Distinction

Often times, the reasons people behave incongruently with their true selves is because of discontentment with where they are in life. When the fulfillment that individuals anticipate from a career is not achieved, they become disconcerted. Job dissatisfaction, including obscured opportunities, lack of diversity, financial issues, to name a few, contribute to behavioral changes including substance abuse, suicide ideation, sexual assault, adultery, or simply slothfulness and unproductiveness—merely existing. Also contributing to disappointment with life is duplicity—especially with oneself.

One of the most prolific lies people accept is the need to compete or be like someone else. The reason that replicating someone is such a travesty is you were created an original not a copy. There are no two people on this planet alike; there is no one on this earth like you. You are unique! You've been designed that way. Do you realize that no one shares your DNA?

What do we know about DNA? For one, it contains your genetic code or blueprint. Genetics informally is the study of how parents pass on some of their characteristics to their children. DNA is inherited by children from their parents. Distinctly, the DNA in a person is a combination of some of the DNA from each of their parents. This is why children share similar traits with their parents, such as skin, hair, and eye color, and facial features. In other words, they look like their parents.

DNA is what gives us our uniqueness. This is so phenomenal that according to medical studies, during blood transfusions, it is impossible that the blood or marrow donations will mix with the host DNA. Cells don't readily exchange their DNA except in the case of sexual reproduction. That means that even if you have someone else's blood in your body, it is only temporary because the life span of one red blood cell is only three to four months. A transfusion is designed to provide an individual with enough blood to last until they can produce their own. So while it is theoretically possible to have someone else's DNA in a sample, those cells are eventually eliminated from the body because your inherent DNA knows the authentic you. Thus, you are an original!

So you have dreams; you imagine yourself in this place or that. You know why? That's what's in your DNA. An imagination starts with "image," it starts with a word. You were already destined to be someone of great substance. At the risk of being too technical, although your DNA cannot change, geneticists say your genetic code can be altered by information that is given to your RNA (molecules involved in the transmission of DNA information). So, the problem is not with the "greatness" and "uniqueness" in your DNA, but with your RNA (the information you're processing).

Go back to the discussion about your script. No matter how uniquely and wonderfully made you are, if you are living by information received from past hurts, absent parents, the emotions of sexual assault or the I am *not's*.., i.e., "I am not good enough, smart enough, pretty enough, courageous enough, etc.," you will not go very far because behavior can alter the authenticity of your DNA.

Let's discuss neuroscience for a moment. Neuroscientists' study the way the brain works and are often called people readers. They can look at an individual, observe their behavior, ask a few questions, and by doing so, can read the person's personality grid. This science is so precise that sports psychologists using this discipline are able to spot talent and predict success rates so accurately that professional basketball and football teams hire them to select and analyze their players. One sports' psychologist was so good, he spotted Tiger Woods when he was six years old and Michael Jordan when he was also very young as future sports' icons. Later, these two athletes didn't hire the sports' psychologist because the athletes already knew they were good and didn't need anyone coaching them. But, the point is he knew who they were before anyone else knew them. This has become a lucrative profession.

Neuroscientists have discovered that there are 16 basic quadrants: four separate operating centers in the brain and in each center there are four types of personality wiring. That means there are a total of 16 maps that exist for individuals and every one of those maps neurologically is going to be predictable in terms of the way people think and act. The implication is *everybody* has the ability to operate at a genius level if only they could fully align with the 1/16$^{th}$ pattern that they *personally* have. This is why you may hear someone say, "Wow, she solves problems so quickly" and then another responds, "Oh that's how she's wired." You are wired a specific way for a specific reason—destiny.

The problem is with the methods that educators use to measure intelligence and we've already exposed the fallacies in the IQ test as a predictor of success. You and I were not told that we were intelligent because if you couldn't spell *supercalifragilisticexpialidocious* or regurgitate all the U.S. capitols or name all the U.S. presidents, then you weren't as bright as your classmate who *could* respond correctly, leaving you feeling intimidated, insecure, and sometimes slow or stupid. So in reality, there was more faith in the IQ test than in the authenticity of your DNA, consequently altering your behavior. Yet, the example we just used demonstrates only one type of intelligence: rote intelligence.

Imagine what you could do if you could dial in with greater specificity on the inherent wiring you have to excel. Fulfillment comes when you are working with the wiring of your gifting so that you are maximizing your genius capacity in doing what you are *designed* to do versus exhausting yourself attempting to do what others present to you as your job description or tragically, "what pays the bills." When you are doing what you are wired to do, it is effortless and more importantly, it's *fulfilling*. It becomes very discouraging and exasperating if you are running the course of life as a sprinter when in actuality you are a long distance runner. And that my friend is perhaps one of the reasons you may be frustrated.

Think about the Japanese Oranda goldfish. In its natural environment, it has the capacity to grow to nearly 12 inches. However, put it in a two and a half-inch tank and guess what? It will grow to about two and one half inches. What determines how long it grows? The fish will grow to the size of the tank in which it is placed.

Likewise, you will operate at a level based on the size of the understanding you have of your internal image. The reason you may be in a slump is in many ways because you are bored; you may be bored because you are not stimulated; you may not be stimulated because you are not activated, and you are not activated because you continue to swim in a constricting tank. You, my friend, are swimming around in a tank while what awaits you is an invitation from the ocean. Think about it! What you must realize is that there were one million sperm in a race to fertilize one egg, and you won the race in the one million-person marathon—You are one in a million.

Recently, we saw a documentary on Albert Einstein. When he died, the pathologist responsible for performing the autopsy on Mr. Einstein actually stole his brain. He wanted to see what made this man a genius. Upon dissecting his brain, it was revealed that several regions of his brain differed significantly from most people resulting in his genius capacity. So, you see there is a science to this thought called being "wired for distinction."

Also, consider this. During the first 90 days of a fetus' life in the womb, approximately 100 billion neurons and brain cells begin to form. During the next 120 days, those 100 billion brain cells begin to explode. Initially the connections between the neurons are not there, but eventually there are sparks going on between them. The result, 100 billion cells of capacity start linking together. After birth, by the time you were approximately three years of age, those 100 billion cells, each one of them forming approximately 15,000 stems and creating synapses, were firing all over the place. However, inexplicably, somewhere between your tenth and fourteenth birthday, nature wiped out half of your neurological network. This is phenomenal because what really happened is nature started eliminating all the connections that were not necessary to your destiny. What remained or survived from that vast neurological meltdown were your signature strengths.

When you think of "signature" strengths, think of a signature dish. You may think it is a dish unique to a particular restaurant. However, in reality, a signature dish is a recipe that identifies an individual chef. When you tap into your signature strengths, it identifies the "real you." Your signature strength is the gift mix that makes you unique. Your signature strength is your core talent or ability that once you wrap training around it, it would cause you not only to be distinct but to excel and be ten times better than anyone else, because there is no one else like you.

If you look carefully, you can recognize strengths in individuals. Observing children can help us better understand ourselves and others. Children know what they love and love doing what they are designed to do. They will, in a free environment of creativity, play out their gifts. We read about a little girl who at the age of about three stopped her dad as he was leaving for work questioning him on his attire. Consequently, she began a morning routine of picking out his clothes that lasted for years. She was that good. Her sense of color, fashion, and flare were all present at the age of three. And now she is a fashion designer. Another individual, now the scheduler for a nation's cabinet minister, as a child would create an imaginary desk complete with phone, agenda, and calculator and proceed to make fantasy airline reservations.

Children know they are gifted and they love what they are created to do. We must really grasp this, not only for ourselves, but before we start writing graffiti on the minds of our children trying to make them what we want them to be instead of assisting them in becoming what their design demands.

It's a sad reality that most people were not celebrated or affirmed appropriately while they were growing up for the inherent strengths they possessed, so they grew up lacking the affirmation or direction necessary in their impressionable years. These are the years when children are like sponges; they soak up everything around them including unhealthy scripts. The result: your core signature strengths possibly could be missed—you might not even know what they are.

At least four to six core strengths are inside of you. If you experiment with life, you will find that there are some things that you do with accuracy and ease in which other people have difficulty. The reason your gifts may be masked is when you are doing it, it seems easy for you to do. For example, if you are a communicator, you may think it's easy to talk and if you are a thinker, you say it just comes to you. Well, you must realize that not everybody can spontaneously come up with something with substance to say and say it well. This is a combination of gifts that may take you years to realize that this is unique to you.

Why is it important for you to recognize your signature strengths? Because a signature strength is something that is unique to you; it is a talent that is within you that when brought to some level of skill development, it becomes a tool to catapult you to destiny. Your gifts (talents and signature strengths) always connect you to your purpose. When you discover what they are by practice and by feedback from other people who see what you do well, the more you are going to discover what the purpose is that you are called to serve. That's why it's dangerous to remain a loner. Others often see what you don't or can't see.

Stop and identify two or three of your greatest strengths. If you're having a hard time writing down what your greatest strengths are, what does that tell you about your relationship with yourself? Not only do you lack self-awareness, but it may also identify that you have a higher critical scale than a nurture scale; so again, you're not being your best friend. You have to learn to be your own best friend (TUA).

When you identify your signature strengths either by utilization, feedback from other people, or by seeing what you do well, begin to wrap skill around them because people who have talent in a certain area have an automatic grace to acquire skills; they are driven to pursue excellence. Those skills, talents, and acquired abilities make up the core that leads you into convergence—an ultimate sense of alignment with purpose.

Equally important to identifying your strengths is recognizing your weaknesses. This can be helpful in eliminating undue stress in your life and help you identify some of the disempowering self-talk in which you may ignorantly engage. Think about this: what's the one weakness that's in your repertoire? Here are some *temperament* weaknesses to assist you in answering this intelligibly.

(a)  Anger: can be argumentative, can overstep authority, and may attempt too much all at once.

(b)  You may not listen attentively to others, can be inattentive to details, often prefer popularity to results, and may "steal others' thunder" in order to be noticed.

(c)  You are resistant to change; can hold a grudge, can be sensitive to criticism, and may have trouble establishing goals and priorities; avoid uncomfortable confrontation.

(d)  You can get bogged down in the details, fear risk, avoid criticism, and may have difficulty verbalizing your feelings.

These are only a few examples and are listed to propel you to think about your potential limitations. The point is not to obsess over this, but that once you recognize you have weaknesses (as do all people) commit to working through the LMEs, which emerge to eliminate your weaknesses and to fortify your strengths. You can then begin your journey to becoming the person you were destined to be. This however, can be a colossal task if attempted alone. Your interpersonal relationships can help.

When more of "you" shows up, it also assists in your interpersonal relations. We refer to this as relational capacity, which is simply your ability to maximize the full potential of your relationships. Relational capacity helps you build relationships, organizations, alliances, and networks with a sufficient buffer factor to handle pressures so that you can stay in total unconditional acceptance (TUA) regardless of the circumstances. The key is if you become skilled in building relational capacity, then you can accelerate the process of becoming more congruent (whole). This is essential if you are to operate effectively in life instead of being overcome by the atrocities of life.

Often times, the stress of trying to fit in or to be liked tampers with your healthy relationship with yourself, which in turn can cause undue stress. While those old scripts about you are being re-written and you are discovering the "real you," your interpersonal skills will also be perfected and your relationships will become more selective and meaningful to you and to those in whom you choose to be in your inner circle.

Once you realize your need to build relational capacity, where should you begin? What type of relationships should you seek? It is important to find people who understand the art of affirmation and truth. Receiving positive affirmation from others will help solidify the positive aspects about you: the good qualities you have that are working well for you. Positive affirmation fortifies and balances your attitude about yourself so that something important to your metamorphosis can occur. It will expand your capacity to receive input on the things that will empower you to accomplish your goals in life. The problem with people who are not affirmed is that they have developed a limited capacity to receive feedback because they associate all feedback with pain. Let's talk about the importance of feedback.

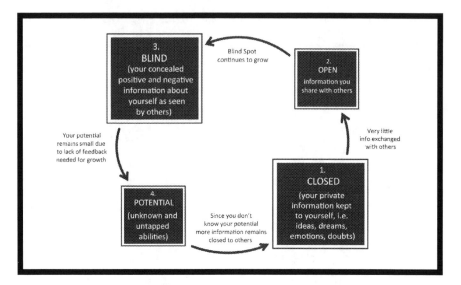

## Relational Capacity Non-Disclosure Feedback Loop

In this diagram of non-disclosure, the four rectangles in the diagram represent windows in your life that reveal knowledge about you. Observe the two windows on the right: the closed window (rectangle 1) reveals information that you keep to yourself and the open window (rectangle 2) reveals information that you have made available to others. Others can see what is in the two top windows: the open window and the window containing your blind spots (rectangle 3). Your blind spot conceals **from you** both positive and negative aspects about yourself that you do not see for some reason. The fourth window on the lower left side (rectangle 4) contains information that no one can see: your unknown potential. This is what gets accessed when you're in that sweet spot (in your zone). Notice how diminished your potential becomes based on how closed you are and the information you don't know about yourself. If you cannot perceive certain things about yourself, you can find them out simply by inviting feedback. The one thing people need the most and often get the least of is constructive feedback on their own behavior. Why ask for feedback? Compare this diagram with the nondisclosure diagram discussed above.

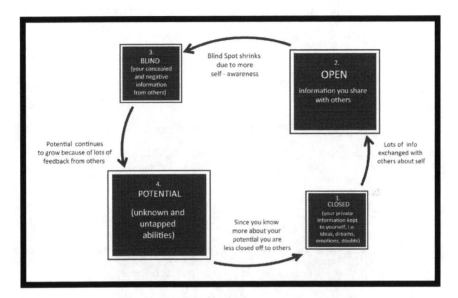

## Relational Capacity Disclosure
## Feedback Loop

Look at how much of "you" increases just by exchanging information (rectangle 2). Not only does your blind spot shrink (rectangle 3), but your potential increases significantly (rectangle 4). If you never ask for feedback, then you are assuming that there is no room for improvement. An interesting benefit of self-disclosure is the moment you disclose information about yourself to someone else, it opens up a window that invites the other person to do the same. When this happens, people begin to drop their masks. This saves both parties from having to expend unnecessary energy to be someone that they are not. It also eliminates the fatigue of worrying about what others might be thinking, or how they might be interpreting what you are saying.

You can maximize your relational capacity as well as those around you. Let's use the example of two people in a marriage. Each spouse must learn how to affirm the other more effectively to solidify those areas within each other that have never been affirmed, or have not been sufficiently affirmed previously. Perhaps they have never put the energy into targeting these areas for affirmation. These areas are easily identified because although they are rarely discussed, they continue to produce discomfort and pain. So, the moment that one person does this, the other person will feel it, and their capacity to handle what was perceived as negative feedback will be perceived as positive feedback. (However, this must be done patiently and compassionately).

When this positive affirmation is exchanged, it opens up the window of opportunity for closed information to be released and light floods into that window. Once both people feel safe, secure, nurtured and affirmed, it is time to ask each other for feedback.

That's why feedback is important. One of the deceptions in life is to be alone and "bear it alone." Feedback is the one thing in which we need the most, yet get the least. Without proper feedback, it is impossible to grow and your progress toward congruence will be hindered, if not abandoned altogether. So affirmation is a powerful tool to increase your willingness to receive feedback, which in turn helps you to remove whatever might be blocking your journey toward congruence and added stress in your life.

Self-awareness, personal responsibility, and sustained motivation are the keys to managing yourself. Empathy and trust (which is what we've been addressing here) are the two keys to exercising emotional intelligence towards other people (a catalyst to your growth and development). This process holds true from your relationship with your spouse and family members all the way through your organizational and career relationships. You can expand the relational capacity between individuals or in a group setting by increasing self-disclosure and making a ruthless commitment for feedback that will produce powerful affirmation in you and those around you. This disclosure and subsequent feedback (to the right person[s]), will calm the volcano before it has the opportunity to erupt.

Consider the misguided message of this quote recited at the end of a popular television program, "Confession is always weakness. The grave soul keeps its own secrets, and takes its own punishment in silence." Someone missed the boat here! This thought is deceivingly deceptive and dangerous. My friend, you must allow "someone in" because there is always safety in a multitude of counselors. Isolation means everything remains in you and creates that pile up principle we discussed earlier.

Take the time to explore this information further, so that more of *you* will "show up" and unveil your uniqueness. This alone is enough juice to make swift adjustments that will produce amazing results in your life.

So, you have some sense of your emotional intelligence (EQ), your relationships are flourishing, now we can pose the question: "what is the desire in your heart?" "If money was no object, the family is in harmony, education is no factor; you have no personal hindrances, where would you be?" Are you having a hard time? Let us help you; (1) the dream you have, the vision you have, the recurring thought that comes to you at the end of the day when you are daydreaming or you are wishing that you could do this or that, that recurring image is the *desire* of your heart. (2) "What do you care about the most?" You're effectively processing this information on "taking on you" and you are no longer reiterating your past or your own personal issues; you are actually in a place of relative wholeness. The desires that keep coming back are the key to understanding your destiny.

If you give merit to your desires and dreams, you will begin to understand why you have ideas and concepts. However, these ideas and concepts will never materialize fully if you operate in a closed state. This is why emotional intelligence and self-mastery are so vitally important. As you recall, there are only two states. You are empowered or disempowered, expanded or constricted, open or closed. When you are in an open state, you enter your personal "Wi-Fi zone" which gives you access to creativity resonant with your talents and abilities. More phenomenally, you are open to the universe to invite you to discover something of potentially significant historical proportion. Jonas Salk, the developer of the polio vaccine and Bill Gates, the founder of Microsoft, the American multinational software corporation, made startling comments about their breakthroughs. They both conveyed that they were simply "open" to a future that was seeking to be made manifest. In other words, because their Wi-Fi was open, they were able to pick up on something that the earth needed—something that was "beckoning them." When your state is closed, for whatever reason, your creativity is minimized. Your talents are stifled and instead of being a level 10/10 (in both passion and talents) and instead of convergence (the place where your gifts, talents, and acquired skills combine with your ultimate sense of purpose), you simply exist. Well, this no longer has to be your confession (secret or open).

The world is missing out on your greatness. It's time for you to get off the bench or stop cheerleading for everyone else. It's time to come from the sidelines, where you've been parked for years because of your past. You have now been armed with enough information to come out of your stupor or disillusionment. You can now conquer your personal mountain and enter your Wi-Fi zone where your gifts and talents have been chomping at the bit to bring you the life of your dreams. The ocean awaits you and by golly you can now swim. You can hit the ball out of the park and we're waiting to cheer you on! And suicidal thoughts, maladaptive behaviors, disillusionment, or "being stuck in life," all become a thing of the past—not even an option. You're ready for not only LIFE, but also, the LIFE of your dreams!

# Appendix 1

# Chapter Review & Study Guide
(Food for Thought)

# Chapter 1: Suicide is not an Option

Rehearse 1-3 in the first person.

1. Always remember that I am gifted with an ability to make a positive impact on those around me and in the world.
2. I have a secret admirer who loves me and who thinks that I am important.
3. If I decide to remove myself from the equation of life, who will take care of the part that life has assigned to me?
4. Suicide is your choice, but homicide is someone else's choice for you. Always take an inventory of your thoughts daily to ensure that someone else's thoughts do not become your choices at some point in your future, because suicides are really homicides.
5. Is your definition of perfection someone else's idea?
6. Who told you that you did not matter?
7. The scales of life are not imbalanced because the negatives outweigh the positives, there is more to be gained when things don't always turn out the way we thought it would. It provides you an opportunity to find out which ingredients are missing.
8. When you looked in the mirror this morning, did you see that winner looking back at you?

Notes:

Notes:

# Chapter Two: *EQ* Trumps *IQ*

1. A man who cannot control his spirit is like a city without a wall and a man that rules his spirit is considered a genius.
2. If you had $1,000 for each moment during a day that you accomplished something that you didn't feel like doing, how much money would you have? Ching-ching.
3. Remember to check your emotional gauges often so that you can know where you are at all times.
4. Never allow your emotions to add value where value does not exist.

Notes:

# Chapter Three: Understanding "Your" Personal Triad

1.  Remember "The Three Amigos"—Focus, Self-Talk, and Physiology, for they have been with you longer than you think.

2.  Combined together as one, they are like the song that you may not sing every day, but once you hear the tune, immediately you begin to sing the words to the song because it triggered something in you that was already there.

3.  What comes at you is not as dangerous as what comes out of you.

4.  Remember you are the one who gives power, meaning, and definition to your life—it's always good to have others' inputs, but always remember you are the one who gives yourself final approval.

Notes:

# Chapter Four: Digging Below the Surface

1.  Is today one of those days that you feel you need a change of scenery, when in reality you need a change of mind?

2.  There is one thing that scenery and you have in common. What you observe in the scenery around you may have been planted by someone unknown to you and what you observe about you may be thoughts that were planted by someone unknown to you. Who is the author of the image that you see when you close your eyes?

3.  The only thing that changes when you bury your head in the sand is that you get sand in your hair and the same results in your life.

4.  Sometimes we are reluctant to dig deep into our past history because we are afraid of what we might discover. If only the Captain on the Titanic had known how big that iceberg was, he could have saved many lives.

5.  The only thing frightening about the unknown is the unknown. The only thing frightening about darkness is the absence of light.

Notes:

Notes:

# Chapter Five: Not All Contradictions are Bad

1. Pain is not weakness leaving you; pain is telling you that there is something wrong with you that demands your attention.

2. Do you understand why air pressure is so vital to fixing a flat tire? It's because before this leak can be fixed, it must be discovered.

3. Pressures in life introduce you to the leaks in your life. If you discover that you have a leak, then that explains why life has become such a bumpy ride; fix the flat.

Notes:

# Chapter Six: The Benefits of an Empowered State

If you possess a car, then you are familiar with all of the different gauges located on the dashboard of your vehicle. They are there so that you can be aware of the condition of your vehicle at all times. When your "Engine Check Light" comes on, it is a sure indication that your car will eventually break down if you ignore that light. Eventually something internal will be damaged and you will require the assistance of a "tow" because your vehicle is now in a disempowered state. Likewise:

1. Always pay attention to your "Emotional Check Light." It is a true indication that something internal will be damaged if that light is ignored, and then you will find yourself broken down in life.

2. When your emotional state changes, you are the first person to be notified. Your internal gauges will let you know.

3. Always remember that whenever a bad traffic accident occurs, there is a high probability that someone will call 911 because of an injury. When your state changes, you must always be the one who dials 911-SELF.

4. Anything perceived as real will produce the same emotions as when it occurs. The adrenalin rush produced by almost having an accident is the same as having an accident. Premeditation produces the same emotions as the very act itself. "All the days of the desponding and afflicted are made evil by anxious thoughts and forebodings, but he who has a glad heart has a continual feast, regardless of circumstances." Again, remember your "Emotional Check Light."

Notes:

# Chapter Seven: The Triad of Transformation

If someone has a drug addiction, going to a rehabilitation center may cleanse their system of those drugs, but not necessarily their mind of "why they used the drug," their mindset. A mindset is software that programs the brain to function in a certain way after you have been predisposed to information. The mind understands or adds value to what it hears, and the brain inevitably accepts the meanings as the way to function.

Transformation is a revelation of new information that produces a new mindset that reprograms the brain and produces a new you that you have never known before.

1. Ask yourself if this information is inherent in your DNA/ bloodline, or is it inherent in your present behavior.
2. All of the education that you have learned thus far was taught to you by someone. Consider this thought, what if everything that you know about you is someone else's' mindset that has been running in your life since childhood?
3. You must ask yourself this question about you, "Am I living my life according to someone else's mindset—" or what the book refers to as someone else's script?
4. Why does pressure cause me to respond the way that I do?
5. The only people that are stuck in life are those who refuse to take total responsibility for their thinking and total responsibility for their actions.

6. When you conduct a personal inventory of yourself, you will find that the things that are really driving you are thoughts that you have embraced as your own as being permanent.

7. Why do others opinions matter so much, when you have so much to offer?

8. Remember the power of transformation: new revelation, new mindset, new software to reprogram the brain, and new behavior you have never known before.

9. Transformation says "Your best days are always ahead," because it is an ongoing process that makes you stronger and better.

Notes:

# Chapter 8: Honor Your "Body" as a Weapon

The body consists of various parts closely joined and firmly knitted together by the joints and ligaments with which it is supplied. When each part with power adapted to its need is working properly in all its functions, it provides one with good health. However, one unhealthy or undisciplined thought not only affects your behavior and attitude but it also affects your health.

1. What's on the inside will inevitably manifest on the outside. The body can make clothes look good, but undisciplined thoughts makes the body look bad.

2. Always remember that you are not dressing properly until you dress from the inside out. The best make-up artist can hide that pimple, but there is nothing that can hide uncontrolled emotions. Try this on for size: "All the days of the desponding and afflicted are made evil by anxious thoughts and forebodings, but he who has a glad heart has a continual feast regardless of circumstances." Don't like the way that fits, how about this, "A calm and undisturbed mind and heart are the life and health of the body, but envy, jealousy, and wrath are like rottenness of the bones."

3. Don't spend your time looking for answers in what happened. The answer is always found in the "why" things happened. The crime is committed first and the rest of the time is spent figuring out why.

4. Let's look at "what" as the fruit and "why" as the root. One will never change the fruit until they deal with the root, and at the end of the root is the seed that continues to produce the

same "what's" in life. The question for you is why do I allow what has been happening in my life to continue?

5. We are fans of the television program, "Criminal Minds," and like to figure out who committed the crime. If we don't know what crime was committed at the beginning, then it is nearly impossible for us to figure out why the crime was committed, right?

Notes:

# Chapter 9: Wired for Distinction

Yes, it is absolutely true that you are wired for excellence, just as a top of the line computer is also wired for excellence. It is important for you to understand that just as there are hackers whose purpose in life is to place a virus in that computer, there will also be relationships that can become a virus if you do not maintain a disciplined thought life.

1. Receive instruction in wise dealing and the discipline of wise thoughtfulness, so that you can perform at a standard of excellence regardless of the adversity.

2. Beware of Titanic Relationships (TR). TRs develop when you allow someone to assign value to your life who is not qualified. In other words, they don't know that you are wired for excellence.

3. Remember this, not all of the people on the Titanic went down with the ship and neither will you when you become the captain of your thought life, meaning everything will be measured by the standard that you set for your life.

4. Excellence is conceived out of relationships that are built on LOVE—the purpose of love is to empower others.

5. It's important to hear what someone is saying to you. However, it is more important to hear the spirit of what is being said—the thoughts and intents of the message.

Notes:

Notes:

# Final Thought

You are an integrated system. Don't rely on your memory of this information to sustain you. The memory of a potato will never nourish you. You have to get the potato into your system. Likewise, trying to live off this information from memory will not nourish you. You must keep it before your eyes. As often as necessary, like taking a prescription, go to the chapter you need for the moment, or if nothing else, review the information in the "Food for Thought" section; rehearse it, open your mouth and recite it. It will be "health and medicine to all your flesh."

You are a winner and you will make it!

# Appendix 2

# Testimonials

As a child, I battled feelings of inferiority, depression, anger, and hopelessness, and with neither my mother nor my father being in the picture, and with me living with grandparents who resented my brothers and sister because we had to live with them, I contemplated suicide on more than one occasion. I was fearful though, because of everything I heard about suicide sending people to hell and all that stuff. So I never went through with it, and found refuge in Jesus. I never understood how I got to that place fully until I heard your teaching on EQ. I then began to understand how emotions and thoughts impacted my mental state, whether I was knowledgeable of them or not. I mean, I was a good kid. I never got into trouble or anything. I understand now how me not understanding about where I was mentally and emotionally regardless of what my surrounding might have been, guaranteed that I would have some sort of breakdown eventually.

Prior to my step dad coming to get us from my grandmother's house, I contemplated killing my grandparents and then killing myself. Only God preserved me. Your teaching gave me so much clarity concerning the questions I had during that turbulent time in my life. I can't say that it saved my life because your teaching came much later, but I can honestly say that it did give me the Intel that I needed to ensure it would never happen again.

DM

The concept of EQ has helped me in my life immensely. I have always been an emotional being but unfortunately, it was in the negative way (or at least what I will deem as negative). I would hold in a lot of what I was thinking or feeling and not deal with it but instead brushing it off as if it didn't matter. In turn, this was damaging my heart and even tearing down my self-worth.

Once the EQ message was introduced to me, I began to manage my state so much better. I discovered that the emotions I was experiencing were real and that I had to deal with them if I wanted any personal success in my life. I realized that I could no longer ignore them as if they would go away but I had to deal with them in order to move forward.

Today because of greater understanding of managing myself and my emotions, I am able to pinpoint why I am feeling a certain way, where it came from and how to move forward.

AS

Before experiencing this teaching on EQ, I always knew that I was destined to live a prosperous life. The biggest question was "how?"

For my entire adult life, I thought that if you "put on a happy face," all would be well. Colloquially, this is known as "faking it until you make it." If you are honest with yourself, you will "make it" much quicker than if you "faked it." And that's *if* you even "make it" at all. Having a "happy face" is a small part of a larger problem. The larger problem is a negative thought process.

With more than 1,500 plus words going through the human brain per minute, I had to examine how many of those words and thoughts were edifying and how many were detrimental to my emotional health. If I am not strong emotionally, it is nearly, if not completely, impossible for me to be emotionally strong for others. Through this teaching, I have learned that if there was ever a time to be real with myself, it would be now. Time waits for no one and I refuse to live a life that is anything other than prosperous. My question to you would be how do you plan to live a prosperous life without first having prosperous thoughts?

Because of this teaching, I am a firm believer that if you examine your thoughts, you will have the power to not only manage yourself but also the atmosphere around you. I have become a better wife, a better mother, a better employee and a better individual through this teaching and it is my hope that I am able to change others' lives with the experiences that have changed my own.

KD

What EQ has done for me, most importantly, is to make me aware of my thoughts and to discern where they are coming from. Additionally, to not allow the thoughts (if negative and not affirming) to linger long enough to become a part of me and produce behaviors that correspond with those thoughts. I have always been an internal thinker and tend to hold my thoughts in. I now understand that silent thoughts can hold you captive if you don't know what to do with them. The thoughts that I battled with were thoughts that I "thought" other people were having about me. It could have been because of a certain look or maybe I heard someone say something (that I perceived) was directed towards me or thoughts that because I was not invited to be close to a particular person or group of people, they felt that I was not good enough to belong. Those kinds of thoughts kept me captive for soooo long. Now, I believe I understand that real or perceived, those thoughts could not have taken root unless I believed them to be true about myself.

Even as a wife and mother, there were times in the past, where I felt unappreciated and unneeded and I did have thoughts of what it would be like if I were not in the picture. There were thoughts of suicide, but never to the point of planning to execute suicide. I think it was more self-pity. The thoughts were intense enough that when I went there, it was as if all of the other negative thoughts about everything else in life followed and piled up to the point where it felt like an extreme attack. I really don't remember how I was able to escape the thoughts, but obviously, I was able.

Although some of my friends and family, members had a perception of me as always having it together or being very confident, I was not totally. I wasn't a train-wreck waiting to happen, but still those disempowering thoughts held me captive and kept me from growing forward.

Having negative thoughts about myself and not loving myself unconditionally didn't benefit me nor does it benefit anyone else that I am in relationship with. I think it is very contaminating.

The negative thoughts still come, but now I'm learning and practicing how to be aware of them, expose them and examine them and then put them in their place and make the adjustment.

It is empowering and freeing to have the information on *EQ*. When negative thoughts and feelings dominate your mind, it weighs you down and they are self-defeating and that is way too much power to give anyone or anything. If invited to remain, negative thoughts can be like quicksand, you will continue to sink deeper and deeper until you are destroyed. You will become the walking dead (living, but no quality of life) or it can get you to a place where you do want to commit suicide just as a way out. The way out is not suicide. The way out is by being empowered to be aware of your thoughts and feelings and not allowing them to have control over you and thus your behavior. The way out is to constantly be aware of them and when they are not in line, to make a choice to make the adjustment.

Life is too good and there is a future seeking to be manifested through me!

CC

Perry & Belinda Moss have done their personal homework allowing them to not only facilitate anyone serious about transforming their lives but also personally demonstrate that life to others.

For transformation coaching, employee seminars, or to request the Mosses for a speaking engagement, please call or write us at:

**PB Success Unlimited, Inc.**
**P.O. Box 931**
**Smithfield, VA 23431**
**(757) 371-3482**
**Or visit us on the World Wide Web at**
**www.pandbsuccess.org**

You are guaranteed to enjoy their bold, no-nonsense approach. Their passion will ignite your zeal and your own passion for wholeness and fulfillment. Be prepared *to change*.